**GRADES
3-4**

...the Super Source®
Cuisenaire® Rods

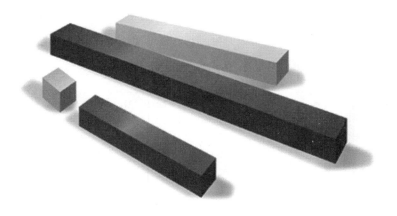

Cuisenaire Company of America, Inc.
White Plains, NY

Cuisenaire extends its warmest thanks to the many teachers and students across the country who helped ensure the success of the Super Source® series by participating in the outlining, writing, and field testing of the materials.

Project Director: Judith Adams
Managing Editor: Doris Hirschhorn
Editorial Team: Patricia Kijak Anderson, Linda Dodge, John Nelson, Deborah J. Slade, Harriet Slonim
Field Test Coordinator: Laurie Verdeschi

Design Manager: Phyllis Aycock
Text Design: Amy Berger, Tracey Munz
Line Art and Production: Joan Lee, Fiona Santoianni
Cover Design: Michael Muldoon
Illustrations: Rebecca Thornburgh

...the Super Source®
Table of Contents

Using the Super Source™

The Super Source™ is a series of books each of which contains a collection of activities to use with a specific math manipulative. Driving **the Super Source™** is Cuisenaire's conviction that children construct their own understandings through rich, hands-on mathematical experiences. Although the activities in each book are written for a specific grade range, they all connect to the core of mathematics learning that is important to every K-6 child. Thus, the material in many activities can easily be refocused for children at other grade levels. Because the activities are not arranged sequentially, children can work on any activity at any time.

The lessons in **the Super Source™** all follow a basic structure consistent with the vision of mathematics teaching described in the *Curriculum and Evaluation Standards for School Mathematics* published by the National Council of Teachers of Mathematics.

All of the activities in this series involve Problem Solving, Communication, Reasoning, and Mathematical Connections—the first four NCTM Standards. Each activity also focuses on one or more of the following curriculum strands: Number, Geometry, Measurement, Patterns/Functions, Probability/Statistics, Logic.

HOW LESSONS ARE ORGANIZED

At the beginning of each lesson, you will find, to the right of the title, both the major curriculum strands to which the lesson relates and the particular topics that children will work with. Each lesson has three main sections. The first, GETTING READY, offers an *Overview*, which states what children will be doing, and why, and a list of "What You'll Need." Specific numbers of Cuisenaire Rods are suggested on this list but can be adjusted as the needs of your specific situation dictate. Before an activity, rods can be counted out and placed in containers or self-sealing plastic bags for easy distribution. When crayons are called for, it is understood that their colors are those that match the Cuisenaire Rods and that markers may be used in place of crayons. Blackline masters that are provided for your convenience at the back of the book are referenced on this list. Paper, pencils, scissors, tape, and materials for making charts, which are necessary in certain activities, are usually not.

Although overhead Cuisenaire Rods and the suggestion to make overhead transparencies of the blackline masters are always listed in "What You'll Need" as optional, these materials are highly effective when you want to demonstrate the use of Cuisenaire Rods. As you move the rods on the screen, children can work with the same materials at their seats. Children can also use the overhead to present their work to other members of their group or to the class.

The second section, THE ACTIVITY, first presents a possible scenario for *Introducing* the children to the activity. The aim of this brief introduction is to help you give children the tools they will need to investigate independently. However, care has been taken to avoid undercutting the activity itself. Since these investigations are designed to enable children to increase their own mathematical power, the idea is to set the stage but not steal the show! The heart of the lesson, *On Their Own*, is found in a box at the top of the second page of each lesson. Here, rich problems stimulate many different problem-solving approaches and lead to a variety of solutions. These hands-on explorations have the potential for bringing children to new mathematical ideas and deepening skills.

On Their Own is intended as a stand-alone activity for children to explore with a partner or in a small group. Be sure to make the needed directions clearly visible. You may want to write them on the chalkboard or on an overhead or present them either on reusable cards or paper. For children who may have difficulty reading the directions, you can read them aloud or make sure that at least one "reader" is in each group.

The last part of this second section, *The Bigger Picture*, gives suggestions for how children can share their work and their thinking and make mathematical connections. Class charts and children's recorded work provide a springboard for discussion. Under "Thinking and Sharing," there are several prompts that you can use to promote discussion. Children will not be able to respond to these prompts with one-word answers. Instead, the prompts encourage children to describe what they notice, tell how they found their results, and give the reasoning behind their answers. Thus children learn to verify their own results rather than relying on the teacher to determine if an answer is "right" or "wrong." Though the class discussion might immediately follow the investigation, it is important not to cut the activity short by having a class discussion too soon.

The Bigger Picture often includes a suggestion for a "Writing" (or drawing) assignment. This is meant to help children process what they have just been doing. You might want to use these ideas as a focus for daily or weekly entries in a math journal that each child keeps.

I used the rods by putting two or more rods together and then I took a bigger rod and put it on top of the other two and tried to see if the two smaller ones matched the one big one. If the big one was to small I would take another block and add it on. For an example: If I had "yellow + light green = dark green + red. You have to add more on!

From: *Writing Equations*

I chose the A spinner first because it was filled with larger numbers, and when I first started playing I wanted to take up as much space as possible. Near the end I started using the B spinner because it had the smaller numbers that I was looking for and a much better chance of getting them in the right combonations.

From: *Rodtangles*

The Bigger Picture always ends with ideas for "Extending the Activity." Extensions take the essence of the main activity and either alter or extend its parameters. These activities are well used with a class that becomes deeply involved in the primary activity or for children who finish before the others. In any case, it is probably a good idea to expose the entire class to the possibility of, and the results from, such extensions.

The third and final section of the lesson is TEACHER TALK. Here, in *Where's the Mathematics?*, you can gain insight into the underlying mathematics of the activity and discover some of the strategies children are apt to use as they work. Solutions are also given—when such are necessary and/or helpful. Because *Where's the Mathematics?* provides a view of what may happen in the lesson as well as the underlying mathematical potential that may grow out of it, this may be the section that you want to read before presenting the activity to children.

USING THE ACTIVITIES

The Super Source™ has been designed to fit into the variety of classroom environments in which it will be used. These range from a completely manipulative-based classroom to one in which manipulatives are just beginning to play a part. You may choose to use some activities in *the Super Source*™ in the way set forth in each lesson (introducing an activity to the whole class, then breaking the class up into groups that all work on the same task, and so forth). You will then be able to circulate among the groups as they work to observe and perhaps comment on each child's work. This approach requires a full classroom set of materials but allows you to concentrate on the variety of ways that children respond to a given activity.

Alternatively, you may wish to make two or three related activities available to different groups of children at the same time. You may even wish to use different manipulatives to explore the same mathematical concept. (Color Tiles and Snap™ Cubes, for example, can be used to teach some of the same concepts as Cuisenaire Rods.) This approach does not require full classroom sets of a particular manipulative. It also permits greater adaptation of materials to individual children's needs and/or preferences.

If children are comfortable working independently, you might want to set up a "menu"— that is, set out a number of related activities from which children can choose. Children should be encouraged to write about their experiences with these independent activities.

However you choose to use *the Super Source*™ activities, it would be wise to allow time for several groups or the entire class to share their experiences. The dynamics of this type of interaction, in which children share not only solutions and strategies but also feelings and intuitions, is the basis of continued mathematical growth. It allows children who are beginning to form a mathematical structure to clarify it and those who have mastered just isolated concepts to begin to see how these concepts might fit together.

Again, both the individual teaching style and combined learning styles of the children should dictate the specific method of utilizing *the Super Source*™ lessons. At first sight, some activities may appear too difficult for some of your children, and you may find yourself tempted to actually "teach" by modeling exactly how an activity can lead to a particular learning outcome. If you do this, you rob children of the chance to try the activity in whatever way they can. As long as children have a way to begin an investigation, give them time and opportunity to see it through. Instead of making assumptions about what children will or won't do, watch and listen. The excitement and challenge of the activity—as well as the chance to work cooperatively—may bring out abilities in children that will surprise you.

If you are convinced, however, that an activity does not suit your students, adjust it, by all means. You may want to change the language, either by simplifying it or by referring to specific vocabulary that you and your children already use and are comfortable with. On the other hand, if you suspect that an activity is not challenging enough, you may want to read through the activity extensions for a variation that you can give children instead.

RECORDING

Although the direct process of working with Cuisenaire Rods is a valuable one, it is afterward, when children look at, compare, share, and think about their work, that an activity yields its greatest rewards. However, because Cuisenaire Rod designs can't always be left intact, children need an effective way to record their work. The "What You'll Need" listing at the beginning of each lesson often specifies the kind of recording paper to use. For example, it seems natural for children to record Cuisenaire Rod patterns on 1-centimeter grid paper. Children might duplicate their work on centimeter grid paper, coloring in boxes on grids that exactly match the rods in size. You may want to have younger children record their work on 2-centimeter grid paper, either to reflect the actual size of the jumbo Cuisenaire Rods that they are working with or merely to provide them with larger areas to color. Older children may be able to use grids with boxes that are smaller than 1-centimeter or may even use a Cuisenaire Rod template to reproduce each piece in the design.

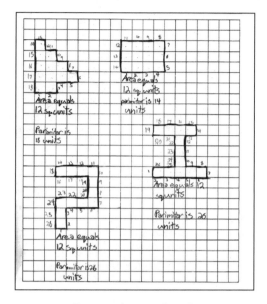

From: *Plots and Paths*

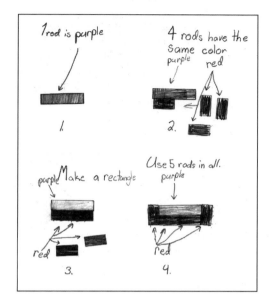

From: *Building to Spec*

Cuisenaire Rods are referred to by the following standard notation:

w = **w**hite	**y** = **y**ellow	**n** = brow**n**
r = **r**ed	**d** = **d**ark green	**e** = blu**e**
g = light **g**reen	**k** = blac**k**	**o** = **o**range
p = **p**urple		

Children often make use of such coding or create their own to describe the relationships they have discovered through the use of the Cuisenaire Rods.

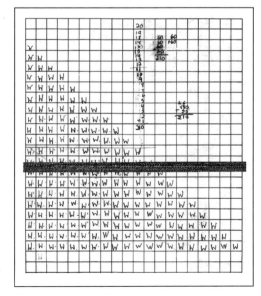

From: *Staircases*

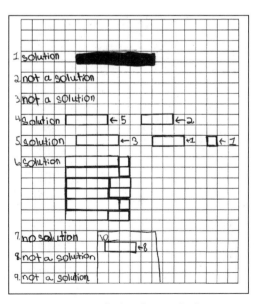

From: *Solution/No Solution*

Cuisenaire® Rods ◆ Grades 3-4 **7**

Another interesting way to "freeze" a Cuisenaire Rod design is to create it using a software piece, and then get a printout. Children can use a classroom or resource-room computer if it is available or, where possible, extend the activity into a home assignment by utilizing their home computers.

Recording involves more than copying designs. Writing, drawing, and making charts and tables are also ways to record. By creating a table of data gathered in the course of their investigations, children are able to draw conclusions and look for patterns. When children write or draw, either in their group or later by themselves, they are clarifying their understanding of their recent mathematical experience.

I put all the color rods I used in making the train in front of me. Then I timesed by two because for each train I had two different color combonations. I had eight different color rods x two = 16 When I counted up the combonations I had listed I came up with 16.

orange rod

B+R	DG+R
R+B	R+DG
W+B	B+W
B+W	W+B
R+W	P+R
W+R	R+P
R+G	Y+G
G+R	G+Y

From: Shorter Trains

You take a a block that equells up to 20, than you take some blocks that equels up to any thing from 1-10. Than you guess how many of one equells up to a 20 bar and you keep on going up to 10.

From: Shopping for Rods

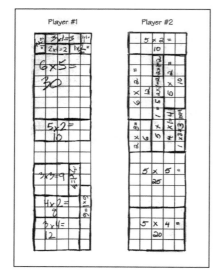

From: Rodtangles

Coler of Burger	Buns	Burger	Buns and Burger
Park Green	10	6	16
Blake	12	7	19
Brown	14	8	22
Blue	16	9	25
Orange	18	10	28
purple	6	4	10
green	4	3	7
red	2	2	4

From: Just-Too-Big Burgers

With a roomful of children busily engaged in their investigations, it is not easy for a teacher to keep track of how individual children are working. Having tangible material to gather and examine when the time is right will help you to keep in close touch with each child's learning.

Exploring Cuisenaire® Rods

Cuisenaire Rods are a versatile collection of rectangular rods of ten colors, each color corresponding to a different length. The shortest rod, the white, is one centimeter long; the longest, the orange, is ten centimeters long. One set of rods contains 74 rods: 4 each of the orange (O), blue (e), brown (n), black (k), dark green (d), and yellow (y); 6 purple (p); 10 light green (g); 12 red (r); and 22 white (w). One special aspect of the rods is that, when they are arranged in order of length in a pattern commonly called a "staircase," each rod differs from the next by 1 centimeter, the length of the shortest rod, the white.

Unlike Color Tiles, which provide a discrete model of numbers, Cuisenaire Rods, because of their different, related lengths, provide a continuous model. Thus, they allow you to assign a value to one rod and then assign values to the other rods by using the relationships among the rods.

Cuisenaire Rods can be used to develop a wide variety of mathematical ideas at many different levels of complexity. Initially, however, children use the rods to explore spatial relation-

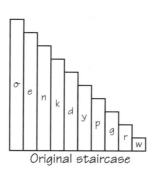

Original staircase

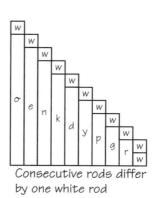

Consecutive rods differ by one white rod

ships by making flat designs that lie on a table or by making three-dimensional designs by stacking the rods. The intent of children's designs, whether to cover a certain amount of a table top or to fill a box, will lead children to discover how some combinations of rods are equal in length to other, single rods. Children's designs can also provide a context for investigating symmetry. Older children who have no previous experience with Cuisenaire Rods may explore by comparing and ordering the lengths of the rods and then recording the results on grid paper to visualize the inherent "structure" of the design. In all their early work with the rods, children have a context in which to develop their communication skills through the use of grade-appropriate arithmetic and geometric vocabulary.

Though children need to explore freely, some may appreciate specific challenges, such as being asked to make designs with certain types of symmetry, or certain characteristics, such as different colors representing different fractional parts.

WORKING WITH CUISENAIRE RODS

One of the basic uses of Cuisenaire Rods is to provide a model for the numbers 1 to 10. If the white rod is assigned the value of 1, the red rod is assigned the value of 2 because the red rod has the same length as a "train" of two white rods. Similarly, the rods from light green through orange are assigned values from 3 through 10, respectively. The orange and white rods can provide a model for place value. To find the length of a certain train, children can cover the train with as many orange rods as they can and then fill in the remaining distance with white rods; so a train covered with 3 orange rods and 4 white rods is 34 white rods long.

The rods can be placed end-to-end to model addition. For example, 2 + 3 can be found by first making a train with a red rod (2) and a light green rod (3) and then finding the single rod (yellow) whose length (5) is equal in length to the two-car train. This model corresponds to addition on a number line.

The rods can also be used for acting out subtraction as the search for a missing addend. For example, 5 – 2 can be found by placing a red rod (2) on top of a yellow (5), then looking for the rod which, when placed next to the red, makes a train equal in length to the yellow.

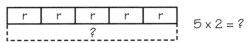

Multiplication, such as 5 x 2, is interpreted as repeated addition by making a train of five red rods or of two yellow rods.

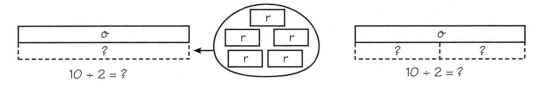

Division, such as 10 ÷ 2, may be interpreted as repeated subtraction ("How many red rods make a train as long as an orange rod?") or as sharing ("Two of what color rod make a train as long as an orange rod?").

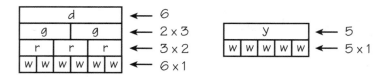

Cuisenaire Rods also make effective models for decimals and fractions. If the orange rod is designated as the unit rod, then the white, red, and light green rods represent 0.1, 0.2, and 0.3, respectively. If the dark green rod is chosen as the unit, then the white, red, and light green rods represent $\frac{1}{6}$, $\frac{2}{6}$ ($\frac{1}{3}$), and $\frac{3}{6}$ ($\frac{1}{2}$), respectively. Once the unit rod has been established, addition, subtraction, multiplication, and division of decimals and fractions can be modeled in the same way as are the operations with whole numbers.

Cuisenaire Rods are suitable for a variety of geometric and measurement investigations. Once children develop a sense that the white rod is one centimeter long, they have little difficulty in accepting and using centimeters as units of length. Since the face of the white rod has an area of one square centimeter, the rods are ideal for finding area in square centimeters. Since the volume of the white rod is one cubic centimeter, the rods can exemplify the meaning of volume as children use rods to fill up boxes. Children may even develop a sense of a milliliter as the capacity of a container that holds exactly one white rod.

Cuisenaire Rods offer many possibilities for forming and discovering number patterns both through creating designs that are growing according to some pattern and through finding the number of ways in which a rod can be made as the sum of other rods. This second scenario can lead to the concept of factors of a number and prime numbers.

The rods also provide a context for the building of logical reasoning skills. For example, children can use two loops of string to create a Venn Diagram showing the multiples of both red and light green rods (which represent 2 and 3, respectively) by placing the multiples of red (red, purple, dark green, brown, and orange) in one loop, the multiples of light green (light green, dark green, and blue) in the other loop, and then creating an overlap of the two loops and placing the rod representing the common multiple (dark green which represents 6) in the overlap.

ASSESSING CHILDREN'S UNDERSTANDING

Cuisenaire Rods are wonderful tools for assessing children's mathematical thinking. Watching children work with Cuisenaire Rods gives you a sense of how they approach a mathematical problem. Their thinking can be "seen," in so far as that thinking is expressed through the way they construct, recognize, and continue spatial patterns. When a class breaks up into small working groups, you are able to circulate, listen, and raise questions, all the while focusing on how individuals are thinking. Here is a perfect opportunity for authentic assessment.

Having children describe their designs and share their strategies and thinking with the whole class gives you another opportunity for observational assessment. Furthermore, you may want to gather children's recorded work or invite them to choose pieces to add to their math portfolios.

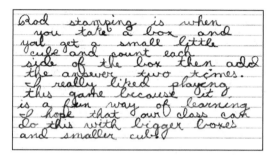 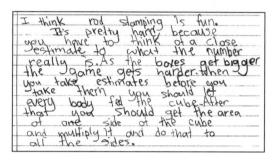

From: *Rod Stamping*

Models of teachers assessing children's understanding can be found in Cuisenaire's series of videotapes listed below.

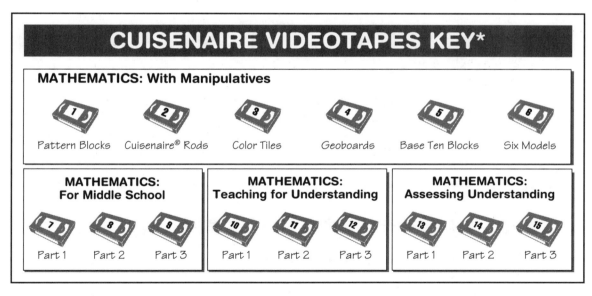

*See *Overview of the Lessons*, pages 16-17, for specific lesson/video correlation.

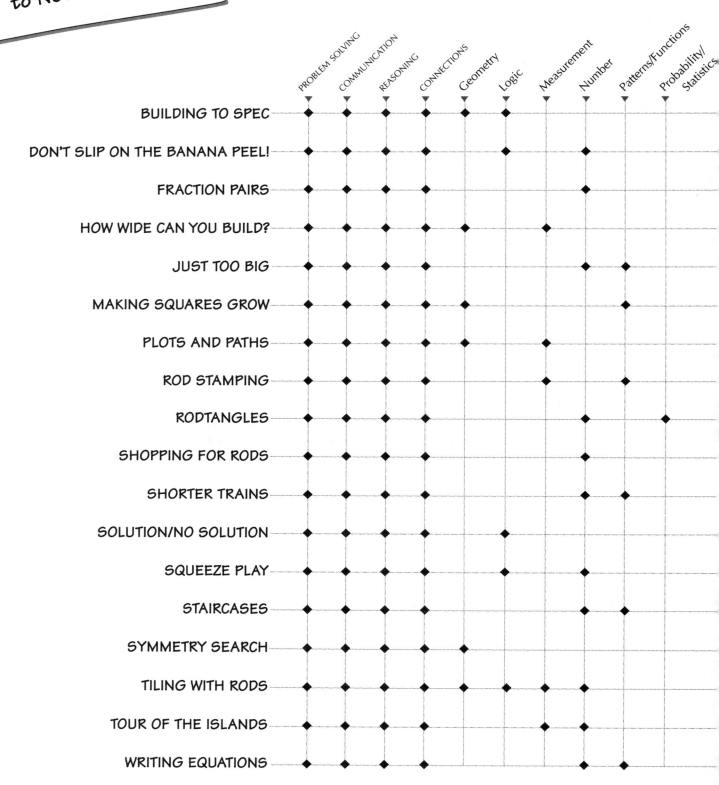

	PROBLEM SOLVING	COMMUNICATION	REASONING	CONNECTIONS	Geometry	Logic	Measurement	Number	Patterns/Functions	Probability/Statistics
BUILDING TO SPEC	◆	◆	◆	◆	◆	◆				
DON'T SLIP ON THE BANANA PEEL!	◆	◆		◆		◆		◆		
FRACTION PAIRS	◆	◆	◆	◆				◆		
HOW WIDE CAN YOU BUILD?	◆	◆	◆	◆	◆		◆			
JUST TOO BIG	◆	◆	◆					◆	◆	
MAKING SQUARES GROW	◆	◆	◆	◆	◆				◆	
PLOTS AND PATHS	◆	◆	◆	◆		◆	◆			
ROD STAMPING	◆	◆	◆	◆		◆			◆	
RODTANGLES	◆							◆		◆
SHOPPING FOR RODS	◆	◆	◆	◆				◆		
SHORTER TRAINS	◆	◆	◆					◆	◆	
SOLUTION/NO SOLUTION	◆	◆	◆			◆				
SQUEEZE PLAY	◆	◆	◆			◆		◆		
STAIRCASES	◆	◆	◆	◆				◆	◆	
SYMMETRY SEARCH	◆	◆	◆	◆	◆					
TILING WITH RODS	◆	◆	◆	◆		◆	◆	◆		
TOUR OF THE ISLANDS	◆	◆	◆	◆	◆			◆		
WRITING EQUATIONS	◆	◆	◆	◆				◆	◆	

©1996 Cuisenaire Company of America, Inc.

TOPICS

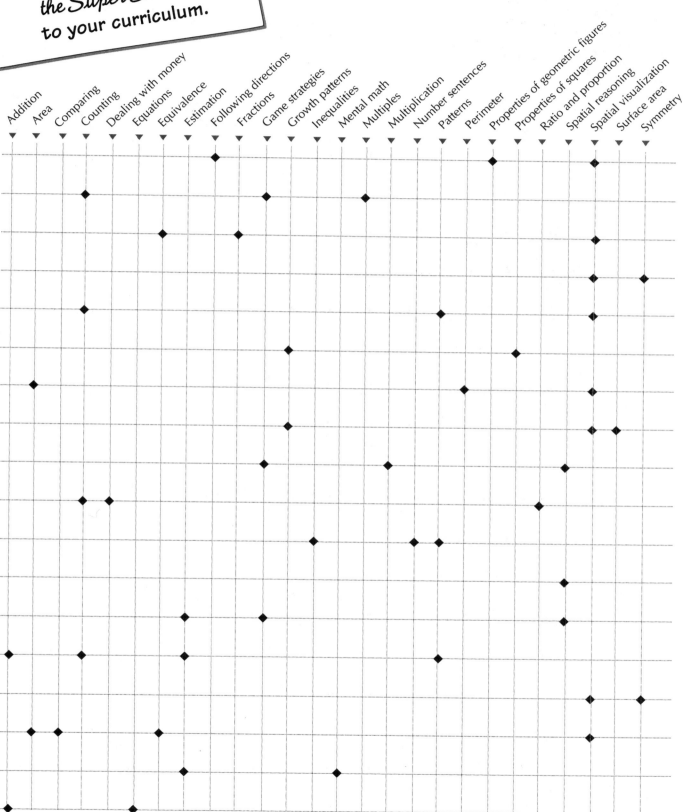

Addition · Area · Comparing · Counting · Dealing with money · Equations · Equivalence · Estimation · Following directions · Fractions · Game strategies · Growth patterns · Inequalities · Mental math · Multiples · Multiplication · Number sentences · Patterns · Perimeter · Properties of geometric figures · Properties of squares · Ratio and proportion · Spatial reasoning · Spatial visualization · Surface area · Symmetry

Classroom-tested activities contained in these *Super Source*™ Cuisenaire Rods books focus on the math strands in the charts below.

the Super Source™ Cuisenaire® Rods, Grades K-2

Geometry	Logic	Measurement
Number	Patterns/Functions	Probability/Statistics

the Super Source™ Cuisenaire® Rods, Grades 5-6

Geometry	Logic	Measurement
Number	Patterns/Functions	Probability/Statistics

Classroom-tested activities contained in these *Super Source*™ books focus on the math strands as indicated in these charts.

...the Super Source™ Tangrams, Grades 3-4

Geometry	Logic	Measurement
Number	Patterns/Functions	Probability/Statistics

...the Super Source™ Color Tiles, Grades 3-4

Geometry	Logic	Measurement
Number	Patterns/Functions	Probability/Statistics

...the Super Source™ Geoboards, Grades 3-4

Geometry	Logic	Measurement
Number	Patterns/Functions	Probability/Statistics

...the Super Source™ Snap™ Cubes, Grades 3-4

Geometry	Logic	Measurement
Number	Patterns/Functions	Probability/Statistics

...the Super Source™ Pattern Blocks, Grades 3-4

Geometry	Logic	Measurement
Number	Patterns/Functions	Probability/Statistics

Overview of the Lessons

See video key, page 11.

Cuisenaire Rods, Grades 3-4

 See video key, page 11.

BUILDING TO SPEC

- **Following directions**
- **Spatial visualization**
- **Properties of geometric figures**

Getting Ready

What You'll Need

Cuisenaire Rods, 2 sets per group of 4

Clue Sets, enough for 1 set per group, pages 90–92

Envelopes, 1 for each set of clues

1-centimeter grid paper, page 110

Overhead Cuisenaire Rods and/or 1-centimeter grid paper transparency (optional)

Overview

Children build Cuisenaire Rod shapes to match a given set of clues. In this activity, children have the opportunity to:

- ◆ construct shapes that satisfy a given set of conditions
- ◆ give and follow a set of directions
- ◆ compare different shapes that may result from the same set of clues

| Make a rectangle | 1 rod is purple |
| Use 5 rods in all | 4 rods have the same color |

The Activity

At this time, you may wish to copy the clue sets and have children help you cut the cards apart, put each set into an envelope, and mark the envelope with the number of the set.

Introducing

- ◆ Have children work in pairs to build a Cuisenaire Rod shape that fits the following set of clues. Pause after each clue to allow pairs time to adjust and discuss their solutions.

  The shape is a hollow square.

  The shape uses more than one color.

  The shape has exactly six rods.

  One of the rods is purple.

- ◆ Invite pairs to share their solutions with the class. One such solution is shown:

- ◆ Discuss how the solutions are alike and different.

On Their Own

How many Cuisenaire Rod shapes can you build that satisfy a given set of clues?

- Work with a group. Pick a set of clues. You will take turns removing clues from the envelope and reading them aloud.

- After the first clue is read, you should make a shape that satisfies the clue. Check one another's work. Your shapes may or may not look alike.

- After the second clue is read, you may make changes to your shape to satisfy both clues. Check one another's work.

- Read the other clues, making any necessary changes in your shapes.

- Compare the final shapes to make sure that they each satisfy all 4 clues. Record your shapes.

- When your group has finished, return the clues to the envelope. Choose another envelope and repeat the activity.

The Bigger Picture

Thinking and Sharing

Ask children who solved Clue Set 1 to post their solutions. Find another area to post the solutions for Clue Set 2. Continue until solutions for each of the remaining Clue Sets have been posted.

Use prompts such as these to promote class discussion:

- In what ways did you change your shape to satisfy a new clue?

- What types of clues did you find hardest to satisfy? Explain.

- Do you think the order in which the clues came out of the envelope made a difference? Would a different order have made it easier to build the shape? Explain.

- Is there more than one solution for each Clue Set? How do the solutions differ for Clue Set 1 (2, 3, 4)? How are they alike?

Writing and Drawing

Ask children to choose a set of clues and order them in any way they like. Then have them show in words and/or pictures how the shape made for the first clue can be modified to reflect each new clue, culminating in a solution that satisfies all four clues.

Extending the Activity

1. Have children create a shape using six rods or fewer. Then ask them to write as many clues as they can that describe the shape.

2. Have pairs of children create a shape and write a set of four clues that describes the shape. Then have pairs exchange sets of clues and try to

Where's the Mathematics?

The sets of clues can be adjusted to suit children's mathematical vocabulary and background. Each clue set has many solutions. Here are some possibilities for each.

Clue Set 1

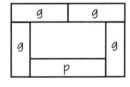

Clue Set 2

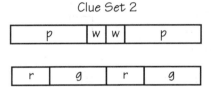

Clue Set 3

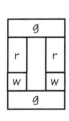 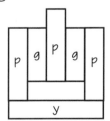

Clue Set 4

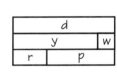

Clue Set 5

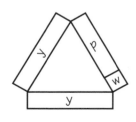 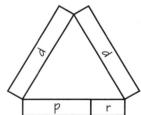

Clue Set 6

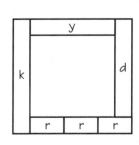 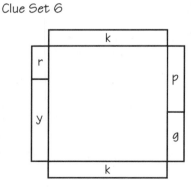

As children give and receive directions they connect language to number and spatial arrangement. Some children may have difficulty when they are asked to compare and check one another's work after each clue is given. For example, a child who follows the clue *Make a square* in response to the first clue read for Set 6 and builds a hollow square with the rods touching at corners like the one on the next page may have trouble accepting the other solutions shown.

re-create one another's shapes. If they create a shape that satisfies the clues but does not match the original shape, ask children to discuss why this happened.

3. Have children work with a partner to build a shape and write a set of clues so that their shape is the only possible solution.

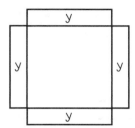 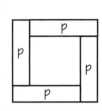 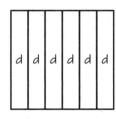

In this situation, children who make the second and third solutions above may have to explain why their shapes are also squares. The give-and-take involved in justifying a construction and accepting other solutions as legitimate can help children become more flexible in their thinking.

Children who intuitively see that a solution is incorrect may have trouble explaining why and let the error slip by. For example, children who use four rods of the same color to make the shape shown at right for the clue *Make a square* may not be able to convince others that the shape is actually a rectangle with one pair of opposite sides longer than the other pair of sides. Such errors will eventually be corrected. Over time, children's explanations will become clearer and more precise.

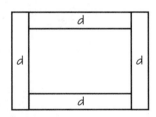

The new information provided in a clue may force children to adjust their thinking and re-evaluate preconceived notions. For example, if a child knows that a triangle has three equal sides and satisfies the clue *Make a triangle* using three rods, he or she may have difficulty figuring out how to incorporate a fourth rod when given the clue *Use 4 rods.* It may be only after seeing another group member replace a rod with a two-car train of the same length that the child can learn how to make changes in a rod shape and still maintain a specified parameter.

The order in which clues are drawn from the envelope may play a part in how easily children make adjustments in their rod shapes. If the first clue drawn from Clue Set 1 was *Use 5 rods in all,* children might choose any five rods of different colors. If the second clue was *Make a rectangle,* most children would have to spend a good deal of time trading in rods to end up with five rods that form a rectangle. Although the order of the clues will affect the amount of time children spend on the activity, a solution can always be found once all four clues are taken into consideration.

DON'T SLIP ON THE BANANA PEEL!

Getting Ready

What You'll Need

Cuisenaire Rods, 6 each of white, red, and light green per pair

Banana Peel game boards, 1 per pair, page 93

Overhead Cuisenaire Rods and/or *Banana Peel* game board transparency (optional)

Overview

Children play a strategy game in which they take turns placing Cuisenaire Rods on a game board consisting of a row of centimeter squares. The winner is the player who can avoid covering the square showing a banana peel. In this activity, children have the opportunity to:

- ◆ develop strategic thinking skills
- ◆ search for patterns
- ◆ use multiples of two and three

The Activity

Introducing

- ◆ Show children a partial game board, one with ten centimeter squares. Draw a banana peel—or mark an X—on the last square as shown.

- ◆ Ask a volunteer to play a game with you after explaining the following: You and the volunteer will take turns placing white, red, or light green rods on the squares until the banana (or X) is covered. The person who covers the last square loses.
- ◆ Demonstrate the game once more with a different volunteer.
- ◆ Tell children that they will be playing a similar game called *Don't Slip on the Banana Peel!*
- ◆ Go over the rules given in *On Their Own*.

On Their Own

Play *Don't Slip on the Banana Peel!*

Here are the rules.

1. This a game for 2 players. The object of the game is to avoid being the player who places a Cuisenaire Rod on the game-board square that shows a banana peel.

2. Players decide which square on the game board will contain the banana peel. They draw the banana peel in that square.

   Draw a banana peel () in one of the squares.

3. Players start at the first square on the left and take turns placing a white, red, or light green rod on the game board. No player may skip a turn or leave a square uncovered between rods. Here's an example.

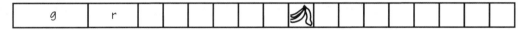

4. The player who places a rod that covers the banana peel loses the game.

- Play *Don't Slip on the Banana Peel!* several times. Take turns going first.

- Be prepared to talk about good moves and bad moves.

The Bigger Picture

Thinking and Sharing

Invite children to talk about their games and describe some of the thinking they did. Ask each pair of volunteers to show where they placed the banana peel and tell who went first and who won. Record this information on the chalkboard.

Use prompts like these to promote class discussion:

- ◆ What did you find out about how to play this game?

- ◆ Does it matter who goes first? Why do you think that?

- ◆ Does it matter where the banana peel is placed? Explain.

- ◆ Did you make any move that you wanted to take back? Explain.

- ◆ On a turn, how did you decide whether to place a white, red, or light green rod?

Extending the Activity

1. Have children draw the banana peel in a different square and play several more games. Have them compare their strategies to those used when they played on their original game board.

Teacher Talk

Where's the Mathematics?

Don't Slip on the Banana Peel! is a game of strategy, not a game of chance. Playing this game helps children develop and analyze strategies. The key idea here, as in a game of chess, is to think ahead and predict the consequences of a particular action.

Most children start by just playing the game with no particular strategy in mind. Later, they begin to see patterns and formulate conjectures about how to win. Frequently, their first conjectures—such as "The player to go first always wins" or "It's easier to win when the banana peel is on an odd-numbered space"—are false. As they continue to play, however, children can test their conjectures and begin to refine them. Then they can propose logical reasons for why their strategy is a winning one.

After playing just a few times, most children realize that if they can cover the space that immediately precedes the one with the banana peel, they can force their opponent to lose. Then the trick becomes figuring out how to guarantee that they can cover that space. If children can articulate that this is what they need to figure out, but do not know how to proceed further, suggest that they try the problem-solving strategy of "make the problem simpler." In other words, if they play several games with the banana peel located close to the starting square, they can observe what happens without being distracted by a multitude of turns. For example, if they place the banana peel on space 2, it's not a very challenging game because the first player would play a white rod and force the second player to lose. If, however, the players now move the banana peel to space 3, then space 4, then space 5, and so forth, they will begin to see patterns.

Eventually, children see that since each player can place rods of lengths 1, 2, or 3 at a time, each complete turn can be held to a total of 4 spaces covered. That is, if Player A places a white, Player B plays a light green; if Player A places a red, Player B places a red; if Player A places a light green, Player B places a white. After a while, children may be able to generalize that they are always counting successive steps of 4 backward from the space that immediately precedes the banana peel. They may describe the winning strategy in terms of subtraction. Here is one child's explanation: "Go one space to the left of the banana peel. Keep counting backward, or subtracting fours, until you get a space that comes before 4. If you end up on the starting point, you go second and cover every multiple of 4 to win. If you end up on 1, 2, or 3, you should go first and place a rod that will exactly cover the space (1, 2, or 3) that you ended up on."

2. Have children play the game again, this time so that the player who covers the banana peel wins. Ask children to compare the strategies they used for this game with those used for the original game.

3. Have children select a different set of rod colors and play the game several times. Then have them explain how changing the lengths of the rods changes the strategy of the game.

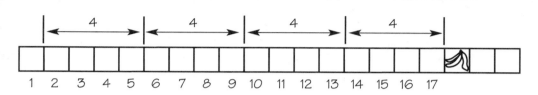

Go first and use a white rod.
Then make sure your rods cover spaces 5, 9, 13, and 17.

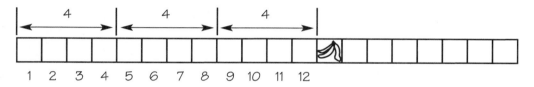

Go second. Whatever the other player does,
make sure your rods cover spaces 4, 8, and 12.

Children may see the key to the winning strategy as division. To find out how to start, they divide the number of the space one to the left of the banana peel by 4 and note the remainder. They may suggest, "If the remainder is 0, be the second player and be sure to cover every multiple of 4. If the remainder is not 0, be the first player and cover just the remainder and then every fourth number after that."

Some children will have difficulty articulating what they are thinking. Other children will be able to explain a winning strategy for a specific location of the banana peel but may not be able to generalize what happens when the banana peel is moved to another location. Still other children will be able to explain their winning strategy but may be unable to accept that another person has expressed a similar idea in different words. If children have suggested both the subtraction and division strategies, this could be a good time to remind them that division may be viewed as repeated subtraction.

If children are having difficulty analyzing what is happening, you might want to designate the space in which to position the banana peel. Have everyone play several times with the banana peel in this square, then resume the class discussion.

FRACTION PAIRS

- Fractions
- Spatial visualization
- Equivalence

Getting Ready

What You'll Need

Cuisenaire Rods, 1 set per pair

1-centimeter grid paper (optional), page 110

Overhead Cuisenaire Rods and or 1-centimeter grid paper transparency (optional)

Overview

Children find all pairs of Cuisenaire Rods that have a relationship that can be expressed in terms of a unit fraction. In this activity, children have the opportunity to:

- explore the meaning of fractions
- determine that the same fraction name can describe different rod pairs
- develop a mental picture of fractional parts of a whole

The Activity

Introducing

- Ask children to find a rod that is half the length of the orange rod. Have them explain their thinking.

- Verify that the yellow rod is half as long as the orange. Show children that this can be recorded either as $y = \frac{1}{2}\,o$ or $o = 2y$. Ask them why both recordings make sense.

- Ask children to find all other pairs of rods in which one rod is half the length of the other. Tell them to record their findings in the two ways you have described.

- Check to be sure that children understand the task and have recorded their findings correctly.

$$p = \frac{1}{2}n \ \text{ or } \ n = 2p \qquad r = \frac{1}{2}p \ \text{ or } \ p = 2r$$
$$g = \frac{1}{2}d \ \text{ or } \ d = 2g \qquad w = \frac{1}{2}r \ \text{ or } \ r = 2w$$

On Their Own

How many Cuisenaire Rod pairs can you find to show the fractions ½, ⅓, ¼, ⅕, ⅙, ⅐, ⅛, ⅑, and ¹⁄₁₀?

- Work with a partner. Find a rod pair in which 1 rod is a third as long as the other.

- Record your findings in 2 ways. Here is an example of how to record a white and light green rod pair:

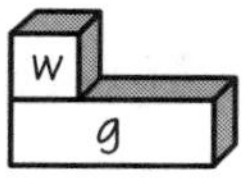

Recordings
$w = ⅓g$ or $g = 3w$

- Find as many more rod pairs as you can that show ⅓. Record each pair in 2 ways.

- Now, look for rod pairs that show ¼ and record each of those in 2 ways.

- Continue finding and recording rod pairs for all the fractions listed above until you think that you have found all the pairs possible for each fraction.

- Be ready to explain why you think you have found all possible rod pairs for each of the fractions.

The Bigger Picture

Thinking and Sharing

Write the following fractions across the chalkboard: ½, ⅓, ¼, ⅕, ⅙, ⅐, ⅛, ⅑, ¹⁄₁₀. Have children share their recordings by listing their sentences under the appropriate fraction. The list should begin to look like this.

1/2	1/3
$w = ½r$ or $r = 2w$	$w = ⅓g$ or $g = 3w$
$r = ½p$ or $p = 2r$	
$g = ½d$ or $d = 2g$	
$p = ½n$ or $n = 2p$	
$y = ½O$ or $O = 2y$	

Use prompts like these to promote class discussion:

- What patterns do you notice for each fraction? for all the fractions?

- How do you know that the list for (name a fraction) is complete?

- Why isn't (name a rod) on this list?

- How can the same rod be used to represent two different fractions?

- Why are some fractions represented by fewer rod pairs than others?

Extending the Activity

Ask children to imagine that a red rod and an orange rod are combined in a train to form a new rod called "rorange." Have children repeat the activity and include the rorange rod when forming rod pairs.

Where's the Mathematics?

This activity can help deepen children's understanding of a fraction as a ratio of one whole number to another. As children place Cuisenaire Rods next to one another and decide how the length of the shorter rod may be expressed in terms of the length of the longer rod, they are modeling ratios that represent unit fractions.

The following table lists all possible answers. Individual pairs of children may not be able to find all these solutions on their own.

$\frac{1}{2}$	$\frac{1}{3}$	$\frac{1}{4}$
$w = \frac{1}{2}r$ or $r = 2w$	$w = \frac{1}{3}g$ or $g = 3w$	$w = \frac{1}{4}p$ or $p = 4w$
$r = \frac{1}{2}p$ or $p = 2r$	$r = \frac{1}{3}d$ or $d = 3r$	$r = \frac{1}{4}n$ or $n = 4r$
$g = \frac{1}{2}d$ or $d = 2g$	$g = \frac{1}{3}e$ or $e = 3g$	
$p = \frac{1}{2}n$ or $n = 2p$		
$y = \frac{1}{2}o$ or $o = 2y$		

$\frac{1}{5}$	$\frac{1}{6}$	$\frac{1}{7}$
$w = \frac{1}{5}y$ or $y = 5w$	$w = \frac{1}{6}d$ or $d = 6w$	$w = \frac{1}{7}k$ or $k = 7w$
$r = \frac{1}{5}o$ or $o = 5r$		

$\frac{1}{8}$	$\frac{1}{9}$	$\frac{1}{10}$
$w = \frac{1}{8}n$ or $n = 8w$	$w = \frac{1}{9}e$ or $e = 9w$	$w = \frac{1}{10}o$ or $o = 10w$

The question "How big is one half?" cannot be answered meaningfully until one knows the size of the whole unit; this is because a fraction indicates only a relationship between a part and the whole. As children look down the list for $\frac{1}{2}$, the idea of a fraction as a relationship, and not as an absolute quantity, is reinforced as they see the five different-sized pairs of rods used to represent one half. Additional reinforcement comes as children look across the lists and see that the same rod can have a variety of fractional names.

Children may approach this task randomly, but once they have completed their lists for $\frac{1}{2}$ and $\frac{1}{3}$, they usually find an organized way of approaching the work. For example, when searching for rod pairs for $\frac{1}{4}$, many children start with the shortest rod (white), place four of them in a train, and find $w = \frac{1}{4} p$ or $p = 4w$; then they move on to the next shortest rod (red), place four of them in a train, and find $r = \frac{1}{4} n$ or $n = 4r$. When they try to repeat the process for the next shortest rod (light green), they discover that the four-car train is longer than an orange rod, so they look no further.

Children who use this method of searching for rod pairs recognize that the denominator of the fraction indicates how many of the shorter rod to put down (or how many equal parts are required to make the whole). That is, if the denominator is 4, they place four rods in a train and look for a longer rod with a matching length.

Children will notice that as they move along in the chart from $\frac{1}{2}$ to $\frac{1}{10}$, the lists get shorter. They will also notice that the white rod shows up on every list. When asked why certain rods are not on some lists, for example, "Why isn't purple on the $\frac{1}{3}$ list?" children may verbalize that $\frac{1}{3}$ means that 3 of one color equal the length of a longer rod. If they used 3 white rods, the length would be shorter than a purple and the next larger possibility, 3 reds, would be longer than a purple. Therefore, purple could not be used as the longer rod. If purple was used as the shorter rod, and three were placed in a train, the train would be longer than the orange rod. It is very important to emphasize that the denominator of a fraction indicates the number of equal parts that are required to make the whole.

HOW WIDE CAN YOU BUILD?

- Symmetry
- Spatial visualization

Getting Ready

What You'll Need

Cuisenaire Rods, 1 set per pair

Crayons (optional)

1-centimeter grid paper, 1 sheet per pair, page 110

Centimeter ruler (optional)

Overhead Cuisenaire Rods and/or 1-centimeter grid paper transparency (optional)

Overview

Children build Cuisenaire Rod structures having a base of one white rod. They try to make their structures as wide as possible. In this activity, children have the opportunity to:

- ◆ discover relationships between rods
- ◆ work with factors that contribute to the equilibrium of a structure

The Activity

It will contribute to the challenge of the activity if every pair of children has an identical set of rods to work with.

Introducing

- ◆ Use a ruler or 1-centimeter grid paper to demonstrate that the width, height, and length of white rods each measure one centimeter.

- ◆ Build this structure.

- ◆ Invite volunteers to come up and select different-colored rods and determine their dimensions.

- ◆ Ask children to imagine that the rods in the structure are glued together and you want to pack them in a box. Ask children how wide the box should be.

- ◆ Verify that the width of the box should be at least 11 centimeters by drawing the structure in two dimensions.

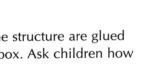

On Their Own

> **How wide a structure can you build that will balance on 1 white Cuisenaire Rod?**
>
> - Work with a partner. Put 1 white rod on a flat surface. This is your building base.
>
> - Using other Cuisenaire Rods, build a structure on top of your base so that no other rod touches the flat surface. Try to make your structure as wide as possible.
>
> - Record your structure on grid paper. Write its width in centimeters, then write the total number of rods that you used.
>
> - Exchange your recordings with another pair and try to build one another's structures.
>
> - With your partner, talk about what you noticed about how rods can be balanced.
>
> - Now, try to build an even wider structure than you built before. Record it.

The Bigger Picture

Thinking and Sharing

Have pairs post the recordings of their structures. Then lead the class to rearrange their recordings by width and have them discuss any relationships they discover from the class display.

Use prompts such as these to promote class discussion:

- What strategies did you use to make your structure?

- Does the width of your structure have anything to do with the number of rods you used? Explain.

- How are the widest structures alike? How are they different?

- What was hard about making your structure? What was hard about building the other pair's structure?

- How did you keep your structure from toppling?

- Which structures are the most appealing to you? Why?

Writing and Drawing

Have children list the factors that make a structure balance. Ask children to provide illustrations where appropriate.

Extending the Activity

Challenge children to make as wide a construction as possible using exactly ten rods.

Where's the Mathematics?

This activity blends a physical science lesson on balance and equilibrium with a mathematics lesson involving symmetry, finding halves, and discovering relationships between measurements.

Children typically begin their construction using trial-and-error. One of the first things they discover is that generally they can place only one rod on

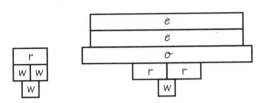

top of the white rod. When they try to place two rods directly on the base, those two rods must be weighted down with one or more rods to keep the structure from toppling.

Such configurations do not have much stability, so children usually abandon this idea and move on to deciding which individual rod is best to balance on top of the white rod, the first layer of the structure.

Children usually discover that the closer they align the center of the rod they choose for the second layer with the center of the white rod, the more stable the structure will be. Frequently, children select the orange rod as the one to balance on the white rod since the orange rod is widest. Further into the process, children may return and choose a shorter rod, such as black or brown, in order to save the longer orange rods for the upper layers of the structure.

When building a third layer, children often discover that if they want to use two rods, they should use rods of the same color and arrange them symmetrically so the weight is equally distributed.

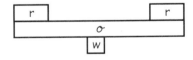 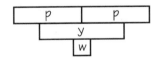

Children also learn that if more than half a rod hangs over the rod that is just beneath it, they must place another rod over the center to add stability.

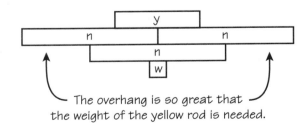

The overhang is so great that the weight of the yellow rod is needed.

After they have added a rod to weigh down the rods below it, some children learn that they can pull the two rods slightly apart and gain additional width. As they pull the rods apart, they need to maintain symmetry to keep the balance.

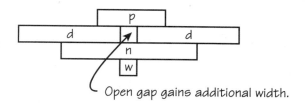

Open gap gains additional width.

As children add more layers to their structures, the balancing act gets quite complicated, and they learn the value of cooperating with a partner. One child may stabilize the structure while the other adds new rods, or both children may each add a rod at the same time. Other children may choose to first build their structures without the white base rod and then lift the structure onto the white rod when they are convinced that the structure will have stability.

As children record their structures on grid paper, they frequently must deal with how to record halves. For example, if they want to draw a brown rod balanced on a white rod and they have used one square on the grid paper to represent the white rod, they have to center the 8-centimeter brown rod on the white rod, causing the ends of the brown rod to be located halfway between grid lines.

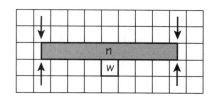

Some children will do this by counting boxes on the grid paper while other children will place a brown rod on the grid paper and move it around until it is centered above the white rod and then trace around it. Other children will draw the brown rod covering 8 centimeters on the grid paper and then center the white rod beneath it so that its ends are located halfway between grid lines.

Creating accurate recordings that other children can use to replicate their structures will help children to see the importance of a clear set of directions. It also models the concept that the results of scientific experiments are valid only if they can be replicated by other scientists.

JUST TOO BIG

- Patterns
- Counting
- Spatial visualization

Getting Ready

What You'll Need

Cuisenaire Rods, 1 set per pair

Overhead Cuisenaire Rods and/or
1-centimeter grid paper transparency
(optional)

Overview

Children create different-sized "burgers" using two Cuisenaire Rods of the
same color as the bun and one rod of a different color as the burger. In this
activity, children have the opportunity to:

- ◆ describe a geometric pattern
- ◆ connect a numerical pattern to a geometric pattern
- ◆ extend and generalize a numerical pattern

Bun Burger Bun	white red white	red light green red
Number of whites	4	7

The Activity

Display a yellow rod inside two yel-
lows and a purple rod inside two yel-
lows to reinforce the fact that the dark
green rod is the shortest possible rod
that "sticks out of the bun."

Introducing

- ◆ Ask children to imagine that two yellow rods are the bun for
  a burger.
- ◆ Invite children to find the rod that could be used as a burger that
  could "stick out on both sides of the bun."
- ◆ Display the burgers children suggest.

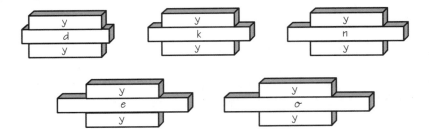

- ◆ Explain that the *just-too-big burger,* in this case, is the dark green rod
  because it is the shortest rod that sticks out on both sides of the bun.

On Their Own

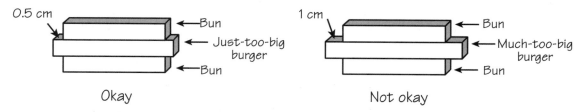
The Bigger Picture

Thinking and Sharing

Invite children to help you list all the just-too-big burgers they found. Ask children to explain how they recorded their findings.

Use prompts such as these to promote class discussion:

- What patterns did you notice?

- Do you think you have found all the possible burgers? Explain.

- Did you find shortcuts for finding the number of white rods needed for any burger? Describe them.

- What size burger would you need to make a just-too-big burger for a bun of two orange rods? Why?

Extending the Activity

1. Have children repeat the activity, but this time each burger is a double burger that is made of two rods. For example, one just-too-big double burger would be *red/light green/light green/red*.

2. Have children make "just-too-small burgers" and compare the patterns they find to those for the just-too-big burgers.

Where's the Mathematics?

As children build "burgers" and compare their constructions, they learn to recognize and extend visual patterns. Some build their burgers in no particular order. Others start with the smallest rod possible for a bun and work their way up to the largest. Regardless of the method they use, most children soon notice the one-to-one correspondence between the burger and the bun. That is, for each bun there is only one possible burger. The ability to recognize such relationships between pairs of numbers is an important notion in the study of algebraic functions.

There are nine just-too-big burgers. The smallest is made with one red rod sandwiched between two white rods; the largest is the orange rod sandwiched between two blue rods. In order to produce a burger for buns made of orange rods, children would have to combine two or more rods end-to-end to make a rod that is just too big, or 11 white rods (11 cm) long.

As children find the number of white rods needed to replace each burger-and-bun combination, they are replacing a visual pattern with a numerical pattern. Their recordings may not be as detailed, but they should reflect the following results:

| Bun ⟶ | white | red | lt. green | purple | yellow | dk. green | black | brown | blue |
Burger ⟶	red	lt. green	purple	yellow	dk. green	black	brown	blue	orange
White rods in buns	2	4	6	8	10	12	14	16	18
White rods in burgers	2	3	4	5	6	7	8	9	10
Total white rods	4	7	10	13	16	19	22	25	28

Children may make a number of generalizations about the numerical pattern from the information gathered. Some may notice that the number of white rods needed to make the buns is always an even number. This is reasonable because there are 2 buns, and two times any number is always an even product. Others may point out that the total number of white rods needed always increases by 3, because 1 is added to each of the 2 buns and to the burger. Still others may notice that the difference between a single bun and the burger is always 1. Children who have experience in finding patterns may make a more widespread generalization, saying, "Find the number of white rods in one of the buns, multiply this by 3 and then add 1 to get the total number of whites needed to make the bun and burger."

Asking children to describe the patterns they notice in as many different ways as they can encourages them to become flexible in their thinking. Help children to see that the numerical patterns they notice are related to their constructions. One way to explain the multiplication by 3 and the addition of 1 in the preceding paragraph is to align one edge of a burger with an edge of each of the two buns. This makes it obvious that each structure has three rods, with one rod always one unit longer than the other two.

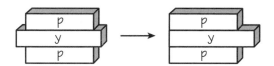

It is important for children to be able to describe a function (a pairing of two sets of numbers in such a way that each number of the first set is paired with exactly one number in the second set) in words. Too often, children think that formulas and rules have no relationship to a situation. Creating sentences such as "Three times the length of a bun rod plus 1 equals the total number of white rods needed" helps children recognize such relationships. If appropriate, you might like to have children take this a step further and write a "shorthand" version of the sentence using letters to represent phrases. For example, using B to represent the length of each bun and N to represent the total number of white rods needed to build the entire structure, the generalization above can be written as $3 \times B + 1 = N$.

Another approach to this function of rod length to total number of whites focuses on the length of the burger rather than the length of the bun. In each sandwich, each of the two buns is one centimeter shorter than the burger. Thus, three times the length of a burger, decreased by two, gives the total number of whites. Symbolically, if R is the length of the burger and N is the total number of white rods, then $3 \times R - 2 = N$.

Still another approach is to look at each rod separately and consider that each burger's length is a bun's length (B), plus one, or $B + 1$. Since there are two buns and one burger, the function rule can be written as $(2 \times B) + (B + 1) = N$.

MAKING SQUARES GROW

GEOMETRY • PATTERNS/FUNCTIONS

• **Properties of squares**
• **Growth patterns**

Getting Ready

What You'll Need

Cuisenaire Rods, 1 set per pair

1-centimeter grid paper (optional), page 110

Calculators (optional)

Overhead Cuisenaire Rods and/or 1-centimeter grid paper transparencies (optional)

Overview

Children use Cuisenaire Rods to build squares that "grow" in a predictable way. Then they use the patterns they see to predict the number of white rods they would need to add to a 25-by-25 centimeter square to produce a 26-by-26 centimeter square. In this activity, children have the opportunity to:

◆ find, record, and extend number patterns

◆ study the set of square numbers

◆ use patterns to make predictions

The Activity

You may have to review the length of each color of rod in centimeters.

Introducing

◆ Use three yellow rods to make a rectangle like the one shown and have children copy it.

◆ Ask children to find the dimensions of the rectangle and the number of white rods it would take to cover this rectangle. Establish that it is a three-by-five centimeter rectangle and that it would take 15 white rods to cover it.

◆ Invite children to add some rods to the rectangle so that its dimensions become four centimeters by six centimeters. Here are some possibilities.

◆ After children have compared their solutions, ask them how many more white rods it would take to cover their larger rectangle than it took to cover the three-by-five rectangle.

38 *the Super Source* ◆ Cuisenaire® Rods ◆ Grades 3-4   ©1996 Cuisenaire Company of America, Inc.

On Their Own

Can you predict the number of white Cuisenaire Rods you would have to add to a square to make the next larger square?

- Work with a partner to build a sequence of squares that looks like this:

Square 1   Square 2   Square 3

- For each square you build, keep track of the number of the square, the number of white rods you have to add to each square to make the next larger square, and the number of white rods in each square.

- Predict how many white rods you will have to add to Square 3 to build Square 4. Then build Square 4.

- Continue to build larger and larger squares and look for patterns. When you run out of white rods, you can use rods of other colors. For example, if you had run out of white rods when making Square 3, you could have used the rods shown here:

- Keep building squares until you can predict how many white rods you would have to add to Square 25 to build Square 26.

The Bigger Picture

Thinking and Sharing

Create a class chart that has three columns. Label the first column *Which Square?*, the second column *Number of White Rods Added,* and the third column, *Total Number of White Rods.* Have children fill in the chart and discuss the data.

Use prompts such as these to promote class discussion:

- What did you notice as you built larger and larger squares?

- What patterns do you see in the data?

- How many squares did you need to build before you could make predictions about Square 26?

- How did you find the number of white rods you have to add to Square 25 to make Square 26?

- How could you find the total number of white rods in Square 26?

- The numbers in the *Total Number of White Rods* column are called *square numbers.* Why do you think they are called square numbers?

Extending the Activity

1. Ask children to predict how many white rods would be needed to enlarge a square that was 50 centimeters on a side to make a square that was 51 centimeters on a side.

2. Have children predict whether or not they can build a 26-by-26 square from one set of Cuisenaire Rods.

Where's the Mathematics?

Square numbers—numbers found by multiplying numbers by themselves—play an important role in mathematics. They occur so frequently that children should be able to identify them when seen in a variety of contexts. This activity introduces square numbers as well as the pattern formed by the *gnomons*, the L-shaped formations of white rods that enlarge squares to form the next larger squares in the series.

The shaded upside-down L is the gnomon.

This activity gives children experience with the problem-solving strategy of collecting and organizing data in a table. The class chart should look like this:

Which Square?	Number of White Rods Added	Total Number of White Rods
1	1	1
2	3	4
3	5	9
4	7	16
5	9	25
6	11	36
7	13	49
8	15	64
9	17	81
10	19	100

Looking at the data, children may notice many patterns. The column entitled *Number of White Rods Added* is a sequence of odd numbers. Children may explain these odd numbers in several ways. Some may illustrate what they did and point out that when they went from the third square to the fourth square, they added a green rod (3) to one side and a purple rod (4) to the top. To form the next square, they added a purple (4) to one side and a yellow (5) to the top. To form the next square, they added a yellow (5) to one side and a dark green (6) to the top. To generalize, they added a rod to one side that was the same size as the side of the square, and they added a rod to the top that was one centimeter longer than the side of the square. So they would predict that to go from the 25th square to the 26th square, they would need to add 25 white rods to one side and 26 rods to the top for a total of 51 white rods added.

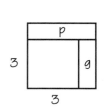
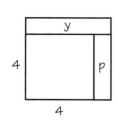
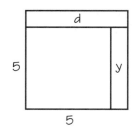
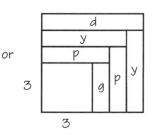

Other children might report that they saw the pattern this way:
As they moved from one square to the next, they added a rod to the side and a rod to the top, each of which was the same length as the square, and then they added a white rod in a corner to complete the new square. They would predict that to go from the 25th to 26th square, they needed to add 25 + 25 + 1, or 51, new white rods.

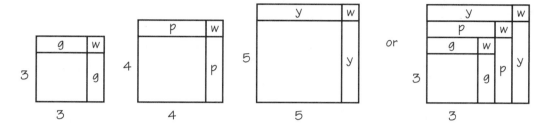

Some children may choose to solve the problem of the 26th square simply by extending the table and continuing the pattern of odd numbers 21, 23, 25, ... until they reach the number corresponding to the 26th square, 51.

Children will initially see the numbers in the column labeled *Total Number of White Rods* as the sum of the preceding number in that column plus the *Number of White Rods Added* in that row. For example, 4 = 1 + 3; 9 = 4 + 5, and so forth. This method works, but is not very efficient when the number of the square becomes quite large. To find the total number of white rods in the 26th square, children would have to extend the chart up to the 25th square in order to have all the data they need to make the addition. Upon further reflection, some children may contribute that the total number of white rods is simply the number of the square multiplied by itself. For example, 4 = 2 x 2; 9 = 3 x 3 and so forth. This method for finding the total number of white rods in any square is more efficient since the answer depends only on knowing the length of the side of the square. Some children may point out that the total number of white rods needed tells the area of the square.

Children should be able to recognize that mathematicians call this sequence square numbers because the white rods can be laid out in a square configuration. You may like to introduce the notation of exponents as a shorthand method that mathematicians use to indicate that a number should be multiplied by itself, explaining, for example, that 4 with a superscript of 2 is written like this—4^2—and means 4 x 4, or 16.

PLOTS AND PATHS

- Perimeter
- Area
- Spatial visualization

Getting Ready

What You'll Need

Cuisenaire Rods, 2 white, 2 red, 2 light green per pair

1-centimeter grid paper, several sheets per pair, page 110

Overhead Cuisenaire Rods and/or 1-centimeter grid paper transparency (optional)

Overview

Using just six Cuisenaire Rods, children make different-shaped "plots" and then consider the lengths of the "paths" that completely surround them. In this activity, children have the opportunity to:

- ◆ compute the perimeter and area of shapes
- ◆ compare shapes with the same area
- ◆ discover that shapes with the same area can have different perimeters

The Activity

Introducing

- ◆ Arrange three Cuisenaire Rods—two reds and a yellow—on grid paper so that the rods lie within the grid lines and at least one centimeter of each rod touches another. Trace around your shape.

- ◆ Remove the rods and show the class your "plot." Have children confirm that the *area* of your plot—the part that could be covered with grass—is 9 square units.

- ◆ Ask children to figure out how long a "path" is needed to go completely around the edge of your plot.

- ◆ Reinforce the understanding that the perimeter of your plot—the "path"—is 16 units by counting and numbering each unit.

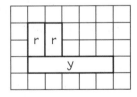

Area is 9 square units.

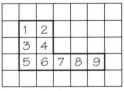

Perimeter is 16 units.

On Their Own

> **What happens when you make different-shaped plots with the same set of Cuisenaire Rods?**
>
> - Work with a partner. Use these Cuisenaire Rods: 2 whites, 2 reds, 2 light greens.
>
> - Use all 6 rods to create a plot. Place the rods on grid paper so that they lie within the lines and every rod touches at least 1 centimeter of another rod.
>
>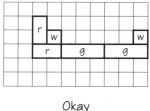
>
> Okay
>
>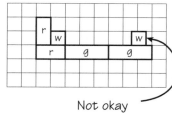
>
> Not okay
> (These rods touch only at a corner.)
>
> Not okay
> (This white rod is not within grid lines.)
>
> - Trace around the outside of the plot to record it. Find the area of your plot by counting the squares inside the outline.
>
> - Find the perimeter of your plot, or the length of the path needed to go all the way around it, by counting the units along the outline.
>
> - Use the same 6 rods to build more plots with different shapes. Record each plot and find its area and perimeter.
>
> - Be prepared to discuss what you notice about the areas and perimeters of your plots.

The Bigger Picture

Thinking and Sharing

Suggest that the class compile their solutions in a class chart or graph. Ask children to cut out their recordings, leaving enough extra paper around the plots to show the numbers they used to figure out the perimeter. Allow children to decide how to organize their solutions. Then, invite one pair to post its solutions. Ask other pairs to add solutions that are not already posted.

Use prompts like these to promote class discussion:

- What do you notice about your solutions?
- What do all of these plots have in common? How do the plots differ?
- Are there any plots missing? Explain.
- How did you create new plots?
- What is the shortest possible perimeter? What is the longest?
- How are plots with the same-length paths the same? How are they different?
- Can every path surround at least two plots of different shapes? Explain.

Writing

Ask children to describe how they would arrange their rods if they wanted to make the shortest possible path around a plot. Have them explain their reasoning.

Teacher Talk

Where's the Mathematics?

Using the notions of grass covering a plot to describe area and a path to go around the plot to describe perimeter helps children use familiar images to distinguish between the concepts of area and perimeter. By using the same set of Cuisenaire Rods to build different plots and then finding the area and perimeter of each, children reinforce their understanding of the meaning of area and perimeter. Children's results help them focus on a bigger idea: Different shapes can have the same area, yet different perimeters.

With this particular collection of rods—two whites, two reds, and two light greens—every plot has an area of 12 square units, or 12 square centimeters. All even perimeters from 14 to 26 units (centimeters) are possible. Here are some possible solutions:

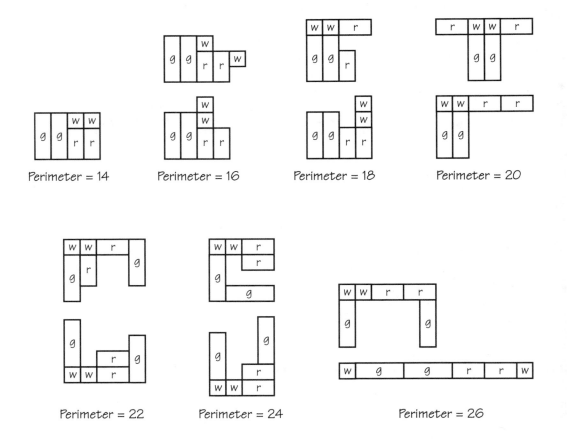

Extending the Activity

Have children repeat the activity using a different set of rods.

The smallest perimeter, 14, occurs when the plot is most compact. A perimeter of 14 is possible for only one plot, whereas all of the other perimeters can be represented by a variety of plots. Plots with the largest perimeter, 26, are the most spread out. Grouping the plots in order of perimeter, from least to greatest, helps children focus on the way the shapes of the outlines move from compact to spread out.

Children find the perimeter of their plots in various ways. Some count the units, going around the outside of the plot, until they return to where they began. Others find the length of each of the sides, then add. As children search for different shapes, they will become aware that turning or relocating a rod does not necessarily change the perimeter. With experience, children may calculate the perimeter of a new shape by adding to or subtracting the number of units being uncovered or covered as they move a rod into a new position to create a new shape.

Children may wonder why all the perimeters are even numbers. If they look at individual rods, they will see that each of their perimeters is an even number because opposite sides of the rod have the same length. Adding the lengths of opposite sides is the same as doubling a number, which always results in an even sum.

2
1 ☐ r ☐ 1
2
Perimeter = 2 (1) + 2 (2) = 6

3
1 ☐ g ☐ 1
3
Perimeter = 2 (1) + 2 (3) = 8

No matter how the rods are pushed together to form plots, the place where the rods touch each other covers up the same number of units on each rod. Therefore, an even number of units is lost from the perimeters of the rods. Subtracting an even number from an even number always leaves an even number.

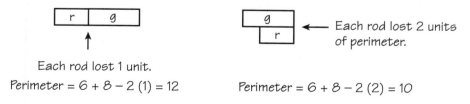

Each rod lost 1 unit.
Perimeter = 6 + 8 − 2 (1) = 12

Each rod lost 2 units of perimeter.
Perimeter = 6 + 8 − 2 (2) = 10

ROD STAMPING

- Spatial visualization
- Surface area
- Growth patterns

Getting Ready

What You'll Need

Cuisenaire Rods, 1 set per pair
Ink pad (optional for *Introducing*)

Overview

Children pretend to "stamp" Cuisenaire Rods with "glow-in-the-dark" ink. Then they look for patterns in the data they collect. In this activity, children have the opportunity to:

- ◆ explore surface area
- ◆ make predictions about the surface area of any size rod
- ◆ use spatial reasoning

The Activity

Children sometimes do not realize it takes 10 stamps because they forget to include the ends or the bottom of the rod.

Introducing

- ◆ Show children an ink pad, a white rod, and a red rod.
- ◆ Tell children to pretend that this is a "glow-in-the dark" ink pad and that you are going to press the white rod into the ink and use it as a stamp.
- ◆ Ask how many stamps it would take to cover the red rod completely if the stamps do not overlap and have no spaces between them.
- ◆ Model volunteers' suggestions.
- ◆ Establish that the red rod requires 10 stamps.

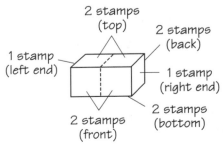

2 stamps (top)
2 stamps (back)
1 stamp (left end)
1 stamp (right end)
2 stamps (front)
2 stamps (bottom)

On Their Own

How many stamps, each the size of a white Cuisenaire Rod, would you need to completely cover a rod of any color?

- Pretend you have a "glow-in-the-dark" ink pad and you are going to use a white rod to stamp each different-length rod. The stamps may neither overlap nor have spaces between them. Here is an example.

  The red rod would need 10 stamps. Here's why:

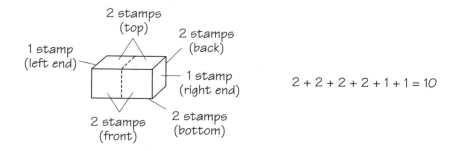

$$2 + 2 + 2 + 2 + 1 + 1 = 10$$

- Stamp a rod of each color. For each, record the number of stamps it took to cover the rod.

- Look for patterns in your results.

The Bigger Picture

Thinking and Sharing

Make a two-column table on the chalkboard. Head the first column, *Rod Color.* Under it, list the rods according to color, from smallest to largest. Label the second column *Number of Stamps.* Have volunteers help you fill in the second column. If there are disagreements, allow children to check their results with the rods.

Use prompts like these to promote class discussion:

- What patterns do you notice?
- How did you keep track of your data?
- Could you predict the number of stamps for any rod without actually stamping it? Explain.
- Imagine a long rod that is three times the length of an orange Cuisenaire Rod. How can you predict the number of stamps needed to cover it?

If appropriate for your children, explain that they have been measuring the surface area of each rod and that each stamp represents a unit of measurement called a square centimeter.

Writing

Ask children to predict how many times they would have to stamp a rod the length of a red rod and an orange rod glued together at the ends. Have them explain their thinking.

Extending the Activity

1. Have children repeat the activity, this time pretending that the longer side of the red rod is the stamp. Ask children to compare their new data to their original results.

Where's the Mathematics?

Rod Stamping provides children with the opportunity to explore surface area before encountering a formal mathematical definition or formula. As they manipulate the rods, children intuitively learn that *surface area* is the "covering" of all sides, including the ends, of a rectangular prism.

Children usually begin by selecting a rod, then counting the stamps as they move a white rod around the surfaces of their chosen rod. Before long, many notice that (a) each rod has four sides, each the same length, and requires the same number of stamps, and (b) each rod has two sides, or ends, each of which requires only one stamp. Using this information, children can simplify their counting strategy to counting the length of one side of a given rod, multiplying by four, then adding two.

The number of stamps needed for each rod is as follows:

Rod Color	Number of Stamps
w	6
r	10
g	14
p	18
y	22
d	26
k	30
n	34
e	38
o	42

The data show that the number of stamps needed (the surface area) increases by 4 as the lengths of the rods increase. To explain this, some children might imagine cutting a rod in the middle, stretching it apart, and inserting one white rod, thus adding 4 square centimeters.

2. Display Jumbo Cuisenaire Rods, or describe them to children. Each jumbo rod is based on a 2-centimeter measurement. (The white rod, for example, measures 2 centimeters along each edge; the orange rod measures 2 centimeters along the edges at the ends and is 20 centimeters long.) Ask children to chart the results of using a white rod to stamp each of the jumbo rods. Suggest that they look for a way to use the data they have already collected to do this.

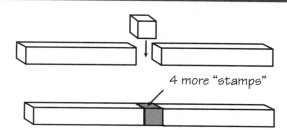

4 more "stamps"

Others might see it as adding a white rod to one end. In this case, the "stamp" at one end is eliminated, but five new ones are added.

While working with increasingly longer rods, children may realize that all the rods have two ends and that only the length is changing. Taking this further, some children may verbalize that the number of stamps needed to cover any rod is always two more than four times the length of the rod. If appropriate, discuss writing this generalization symbolically. If N represents the length of a rod and S represents the number of stamps, then $4 \times N + 2 = S$.

To find the number of stamps, or the surface area, for a rod three times as long as an orange rod, some children will look at the chart and see that one orange rod requires 42 stamps. A rod three times as long should take $42 + 42 + 42$, or 3×42, stamps minus 2 stamps at each place the rods join, for a total of 122 stamps.

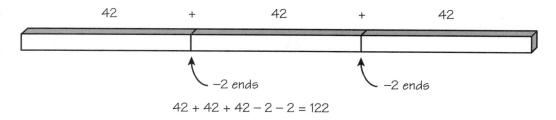

42   +   42   +   42

−2 ends   −2 ends

$42 + 42 + 42 - 2 - 2 = 122$

Other children may continue to use the pattern they discovered on the chart. They might reason that if each orange rod is 10 stamps long, each long side of the 3-car train needs 30 stamps. Multiplying 30 by 4 and adding 2 gives the required number of stamps.

RODTANGLES

- **Multiplication**
- **Spatial reasoning**
- **Game strategies**

Getting Ready

What You'll Need

Cuisenaire Rods, 2 sets per pair

Rodtangles grids, 1 per pair, page 94

Rodtangles Spinner A, 1 per pair, page 95

Rodtangles Spinner B, 1 per pair, page 96

Overhead Cuisenaire Rods and/or *Rodtangles* grid transparency (optional)

Overview

In this game for two players, children use spinners to determine the color and number of Cuisenaire Rods to place on a rectangular grid in an effort to be first to completely cover the grid. In this activity, children have the opportunity to:

- ◆ develop strategies based on probability and spatial reasoning
- ◆ develop number sense about factors and products
- ◆ relate concepts of multiplication and area of rectangles
- ◆ develop strategic thinking skills

The Activity

Introducing

- ◆ Show children *Rodtangles* Spinners A and B. Explain that an outcome of Spinner A will indicate which Cuisenaire Rod to choose and that an outcome of Spinner B will indicate how many of that rod to choose.

- ◆ Invite a volunteer to spin each spinner. Demonstrate how to use the results to form a rectangle. For example, if the outcome of Spinner A is purple and the outcome of Spinner B is 2, take two purple rods. Place them side by side on grid paper and trace around the rods.

- ◆ Write 4 x 2 = 8 inside the rectangle you just drew. Ask children why you picked those numbers.

- ◆ Establish that 4 is one dimension, 2 is the other, and 8 is the number of squares in the rectangle.

- ◆ Call on several more volunteers to use the outcomes of the spinners to form rectangles.

- ◆ Tell children they will be playing a game called *Rodtangles*.

- ◆ Go over the game rules given in *On Their Own*.

On Their Own

Play *Rodtangles!*

Here are the rules.

1. This is game for 2 players. The object of the game is to be the first player to completely cover his or her 5-by-20 grid.

2. Players take turns. A player gets 2 spins of a spinner. The player decides on each turn whether to use Spinner A, Spinner B, or a combination of the 2 spinners.

3. The outcome of the first spin tells which Cuisenaire Rod to take, and the outcome of the second spin tells how many of that rod to take. For example, if the player spins light green on Spinner A and 2 on Spinner B, the player takes 2 light green rods.

   A   B

4. The player places the rods side by side to form a rectangle and traces that rectangle anywhere on the grid.

5. The player then writes, inside the rectangular outline, the multiplication sentence that shows the length and width of the rectangle.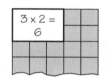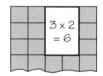

6. If the rectangle formed by the rods is too large to fit on the space left on the grid, the player loses the turn.

7. Play continues until 1 player completely covers his or her grid.

- Play several games of *Rodtangles*. Look for winning strategies.

The Bigger Picture

Thinking and Sharing

Invite children to talk about their games and describe some of the thinking they did.

Use prompts like these to promote class discussion:

- How did you decide which spinners to use on a turn?
- How did you decide where on your grid to draw the rectangle?
- Were there any spins that could never be used no matter when they came up in the game? If so, which ones?
- Did you ever choose a position for your rods, draw the outline, then wish you had put the outline somewhere else? Explain.

Extending the Activity

1. Have children play *Rodtangles* again, this time playing on a 10-by-10-centimeter grid.

Teacher Talk

Where's the Mathematics?

This game provides an engaging way for children to practice their multiplication facts while developing some strategies based on probability and spatial reasoning.

Many children do not initially understand the strategy behind choosing which spinner to use. At first, children think they should always select Spinner A in order to maximize the length and number of rods that they may use. While this strategy works well at the beginning of the game when there are large spaces to cover, it does not work as well toward the end of the game when small rectangles are left. Children who switch to Spinner B increase their chances of spinning a small number of short rods to fit into the small spaces left near the end of the game and may avoid losing their turn. For example, the chance of spinning 1 white rod (1 x 1 = 1) using only Spinner A is 1 out of 36 ($\frac{1}{6}$ x $\frac{1}{6}$) whereas it is 1 out of 9 ($\frac{1}{3}$ x $\frac{1}{3}$) using only Spinner B, and 1 out of 18 using A and then B. This means that the chance of spinning 1 white rod using only spinner B is four times greater than it would be if only Spinner A were used, and two times greater than it would be if both Spinner A and Spinner B were used.

Children will probably not be able to make numerical comparisons of the chances for using each spinner. They may, however, be able to reach similar conclusions simply by comparing the sizes of sectors on the spinners. The sector marked "1" is twice as large on Spinner B as it is on Spinner A, so there are twice as many chances to land on 1 on Spinner B. If there are twice as many chances to land on 1 on the first spin and twice as many chances to land on 1 on the second spin, then there are four times as many chances of spinning 1 white rod in two spins of B.

Children soon learn that a spin of 6 followed by a second spin of 6 will be unplayable because the game board is only 5 centimeters wide. Therefore, some children will reason that if they spin a 6, they should use Spinner B for the next spin to increase the likelihood of getting a rectangle that they can use. If it is early in the game, children may feel that the chances of getting a 4 or 5 will outweigh the chances of getting a second 6 and, in the interest of covering as large an area as possible, they will use spinner A a second time.

2. Have children play the game with this change: Play stops when a player cannot fit a rectangle on his or her grid. The winner is the player with the greater number of squares covered.

In the course of the game, children learn the advantage of packing their rectangles on the grid to avoid leaving small uncovered rectangular regions that may be harder to cover later in the game. For example, if the first turn results in a rectangle of three yellow rods, the third grid shown below would probably reflect the best placement for the rectangle.

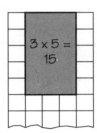 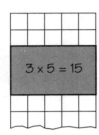 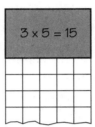

Children who are new to the concept of multiplication will see that a rectangle of 4 light greens (4 x 3) covers the same area as a rectangle of 3 purples (3 x 4) giving them an informal exposure to the commutative property of multiplication. Children will see another application of the commutative property when they see that the orientation of the rods does not affect the total number of squares covered. For example, either arrangement of 3 purple rods covers a total of 12 squares.

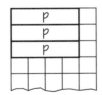 or

Children can also develop some number sense about the relative magnitude of factors and their products. For example, they can visually experience that a rectangle of 4 x 5 is twice as large as a rectangle of 2 x 5. Seeing rectangles of 2 x 6 and 3 x 4 will help them see that some products, such as 12, may result from more than one pair of factors. This activity can also help children make a connection between the operation of multiplication and the geometric concept of finding the area of a rectangle.

SHOPPING FOR RODS

NUMBER

- Counting
- Ratio and proportion
- Dealing with money

Getting Ready

What You'll Need

Cuisenaire Rods, at least 2 sets per group

Shopping for Rods Spinner 1, 1 per group, page 97

Shopping for Rods Spinner 2, 1 per group, page 98 (optional)

Play money (optional)

Overhead Cuisenaire Rods and/or *Shopping for Rods* Spinner transparencies (optional)

Overview

Children use a spinner to find the cost of one Cuisenaire Rod. They use this value to figure out the cost of other rods and then determine a combination of rods that they could buy with $10.00. In this activity, children have the opportunity to:

- ◆ compute mentally
- ◆ work with money concepts
- ◆ use ratio and proportion
- ◆ discover relationships among Cuisenaire Rods

The Activity

Introducing

- ◆ Tell children to imagine that the Cuisenaire Rods are for sale and that the white rod costs $1.00.
- ◆ Invite volunteers to explain why the red rod should cost $2.00.
- ◆ Once it is established that the red should cost twice as much as the white because it is twice as long, have children figure out the cost of a rod of each of the other colors.
- ◆ Show children that the cost of some rods can be determined in more than one way. To illustrate this, display the following:

w	w	w	w	w	w	w	w
n							

r	r	r	r
n			

p		p	
n			

- ◆ Point out that the cost of the brown rod, $8.00, can be found by counting by ones, by twos, or by fours.

On Their Own

How many Cuisenaire Rods could you "buy" with $10.00?

- Work with a group. Pretend that your group has $10.00. You must spend it all to "buy" Cuisenaire Rods.

- To find the price of a particular rod, one of you spins a spinner that looks like this.

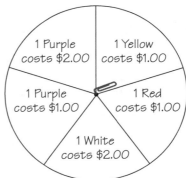

- Use the results of the spin to find the prices of other rods. For example, if you spin "1 white rod costs $2.00," a light green rod will cost $6.00 because it is 3 times longer than the white rod.

- Use the prices of the rods for your spin to answer these questions:

  - What is the least number of rods you could buy for $10.00?

  - What is the greatest number of rods you could buy for $10.00?

  - What number of rods between the least and greatest numbers could you buy for $10.00?

- Take turns spinning until each member of the group has had a turn with a different starting price. For each turn, find the price of the rods and answer the questions above.

- Record your answers and any patterns you notice.

The Bigger Picture

Thinking and Sharing

Invite a group to describe how they spent their $10.00 based on the results of a spin. Invite other groups that had an identical spin to share how their $10.00 purchases were the same or different from the first group's. Continue to invite groups to share their results until every group has reported.

Use prompts such as these to promote class discussion:

- How did you use the cost of one rod to find the cost of the other rods?

- If the spinner showed ———, then how much would a ——— (name a color) rod cost? Explain.

- What did you do to find out which rods and how many of each would cost you $10.00?

- Can different combinations of rods cost the same? Explain.

- What patterns did you notice?

Writing and Drawing

Ask children to pretend that they work for the company that makes Cuisenaire Rods. Have them design an advertisement that includes a price list for the rods based on the fact that one yellow rod costs $0.75.

Where's the Mathematics?

By starting with an assigned value for one Cuisenaire Rod and using that value to find the cost of other rods, children use proportional reasoning based on their understanding of the relative lengths of the rods. In four of the spinner outcomes, this proportional reasoning will lead to work with fractions of a dollar. For example, if the spinner stops on *1 Purple costs $2.00* or *1 Red costs $1.00,* then the rods have values in multiples of $0.50. If the spinner lands on *1 Purple costs $1.00,* then the rods have values in multiples of $0.25. The greatest challenge may arise when the *1 Yellow costs $1.00* is spun because then the rod values occur in multiples of $0.20. If any of these amounts seem too challenging for your class, you can adapt the entries on the spinner accordingly. Some groups may find it helpful to use play money to enact parts of this activity.

Children employ a variety of strategies for spending their allotted $10.00. Some will concentrate on the monetary values by figuring out how much a white rod costs based on the value given on the spinner and then making up a chart listing the cost of each rod. For example, when they spin *1 Yellow costs $1.00,* their chart might look like this:

white	$.20
red	$.40
light green	$.60
purple	$.80
yellow	$1.00
dark green	$1.20
black	$1.40
brown	$1.60
blue	$1.80
orange	$2.00

Extending the Activity

1. Have children create a picture or a design with Cuisenaire Rods and then spin the spinner to figure out the "cost" of their picture/design.

2. Add a second spinner (page 98) to the activity. The group spins the spinner given in *On Their Own* to find the cost of each rod and then spins this spinner to find an additional condition for spending their allotted $10.00, or an amount as close to $10.00 as possible.

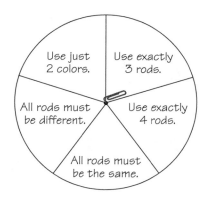

Children then use the values on the chart to buy the rods, stopping occasionally to find out the total amount of money they have spent and using trial-and-error at the end to make sure the amount comes out to $10.00 exactly.

Other children might work directly with the rods instead of concentrating on the monetary value of each rod. For example, they might look at the value on the spinner, such as *1 Purple costs $2.00*, figure out that they could buy five purple rods for $10.00, and then trade the one or more purple rods for rods of an equivalent length until they have answered each of the three questions in the activity.

Finding the least number and greatest number of rods gives children some parameters when looking for an in-between number of rods. This chart indicates the minimum and maximum number of rods for each case on the spinner:

Possible spin	Least number of rods	Greatest number of rods
1 Yellow costs $1.00	5 orange	50 white
1 Red costs $1.00	2 orange	20 white
1 White costs $2.00	1 yellow	5 white
1 Purple costs $1.00	4 orange	40 white
1 Purple costs $2.00	2 orange	20 white

Children might notice that two of the sections on the spinner—*1 Red costs $1.00* and *1 Purple costs $2.00*—have identical outcomes. Children might also make generalizations such as "The less the white rod costs, the more rods you can buy for $10.00" or "You can always buy ten times more white rods than orange rods" or "When the white rod costs $2.00, there aren't very many different solutions." Statements such as these show that children are developing a firm grasp of proportional thinking.

SHORTER TRAINS

- Patterns
- Number sentences
- Inequalities

Getting Ready

What You'll Need

Cuisenaire Rods, 1 set per pair

1-centimeter grid paper, page 110

Crayons (optional)

Overhead Cuisenaire Rods and/or
1-centimeter grid paper transparency
(optional)

Overview

Children select a Cuisenaire Rod and then find the number of ways to make a two-car train that is shorter than the chosen rod. In this activity, children have the opportunity to:

- ◆ relate visual patterns to numerical patterns
- ◆ work with inequalities
- ◆ explore the commutative property of addition

The Activity

You may have to tell children that the symbol "<" reads "is less than."

Introducing

- ◆ Ask children to use their Cuisenaire Rods to make as many different two-car trains as they can that are shorter than the purple rod.
- ◆ Have volunteers share and explain their results.
- ◆ Establish that there are three solutions (white-white, white-red, and red-white) and that, because of the changed order of the rods, a white-red train is different from a red-white train.
- ◆ Discuss some ways in which the solutions can be recorded, such as by coloring a grid or by using words ("white plus red is shorter than purple").
- ◆ Demonstrate how the white-white solution can also be recorded with the number sentence $w + w < p$ or $1 + 1 < 4$.
- ◆ Then have children write number sentences for the other solutions.

On Their Own

How many ways can you select 2 Cuisenaire Rods to form a train that is shorter than a chosen rod?

- Work with a partner. Choose 1 Cuisenaire Rod.

- Build as many different 2-car trains as you can that are shorter than the rod you chose. Here are the different 2-car trains that are shorter than the purple rod.

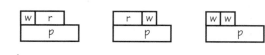

- Figure out a way to organize and record your findings.

- Then choose a different Cuisenaire Rod. Find and record all the 2-car trains that are shorter than this rod.

- Repeat the activity for as many different rods as you can.

- Look for patterns in your recordings.

The Bigger Picture

Thinking and Sharing

Ask volunteers to share their recording methods and their data. Have children decide how to generate a class chart to show all the data for all the rods. Then create the chart.

Use prompts like these to promote class discussion:

- How did you organize your data?

- (Hold up any rod.) How can you be sure that you have found all the ways to make two-car trains that are shorter than this rod?

- Did you find any patterns? What were they?

- Could everyone in the class have a different two-car train shorter than an orange rod? Could everyone have a different two-car train shorter than a red rod?

If children have not used inequalities for recording, you may wish to take the opportunity to show children how to translate their recordings into inequalities.

Writing

Ask children to explain how to go about finding all the possible two-car trains that are shorter than a yellow rod.

Extending the Activity

1. Ask children to tape an orange rod and a red rod together to form a rod 12 centimeters long. Challenge them to find all the two-car trains shorter than this red-orange rod.

2. Have children find and record all the two-car trains that are *longer* than a chosen rod.

Where's the Mathematics?

Shorter Trains provides children with a way to internalize the concept of inequality as they consider which two-car trains to build that are shorter than a single rod of their choosing. Introducing the mathematical symbol "<" gives children the opportunity to use it in a meaningful way. As children read the symbolic representation of their trains, they can connect the abstract to the concrete. Children also learn that the commutative property of addition is true for inequalities as well as for equations; that is, $2 + 1 < 4$ can also be stated as $1 + 2 < 4$. Finally, in this activity, children have the opportunity to see how two problem-solving strategies—making a table and looking for patterns—are related.

Children usually see, without difficulty, that it is impossible to make any two-car trains that are shorter than a white or a red rod. Therefore, the shortest possible rod that can be "chosen" is light green, and it has only one solution, namely w + w. At this stage, children might generalize that the longer the rod, the more two-car trains are possible. They may also see that if the train has rods of two different colors, they can change the order of those two colors and have another solution. Some children may notice that if their chosen rod has an even-numbered length, then there are an odd number of solutions, and vice versa. For example, the purple rod is 4 centimeters long and there are *three* possible two-car trains shorter than a purple. The yellow rod is 5 centimeters long and has *six* possible solutions.

To help children who have recorded a lot of data in no particular order and are having difficulty seeing patterns, suggest that they list their chosen rods from shortest to longest. Data organized in this way might look like this:

g	w + w < g					
p	w + w < p	w + r < p	r + w < p			
y	w + w < y	w + r < y	r + w < y	r + r < y	w + g < y	g + w < y

Now children are able to see that each new line repeats information from the line above; that is, the second line (purple) repeats w + w from the first line (light green), and the third line (yellow) repeats w + w, w + r, and r + w from the second line. Knowing this, children can predict that the fourth line (dark green) will repeat information from the third line and will have some additional entries. For children who have written sentences using numbers instead of colors, the data would look like this:

3	1 + 1 < 3					
4	1 + 1 < 4	1 + 2 < 4	2 + 1 < 4			
5	1 + 1 < 5	1 + 2 < 5	2 + 1 < 5	2 + 2 < 5	1 + 3 < 5	3 + 1 < 5

In looking at their lists, children may realize that the new data for each line is equivalent to the number of ways that a rod 1 centimeter shorter than the chosen rod can be represented. For instance, the new data for the 4-centimeter rod (purple) is 1 + 2 and 2 + 1, which are the two ways the number 3 can be represented as the sum of two numbers. Likewise, the new data for the 5-centimeter rod is 1 + 3, 3 + 1, and 2 + 2, which are all the ways 4 can be represented as the sum of two numbers. Thus, the data for a 6-centimeter rod must have the 6 entries shown for 5 plus four new entries—all the ways to make two-car trains equal to 5—(1 + 4, 4 + 1, 2 + 3, 3 + 2). This thinking is summarized below:

Chosen rod	3	4	5	6	7	8	9	10
Additional 2-rod trains	1	2	3	4	5	6	7	8

With this knowledge, children can verify their predicted entries with data that they and/or their classmates collected.

Chosen rod	Number of shorter 2-car trains
green	1
purple	3 ← 1 way shown in the line above plus 2 new 2-car trains
yellow	6 ← 3 ways shown in the line above plus 3 new 2-car trains
dark green	10 ← 6 ways shown in the line above plus 4 new 2-car trains
black	15 ← 10 ways shown in the line above plus 5 new 2-car trains
brown	21 ← 15 ways shown in the line above plus 6 new 2-car trains
blue	28 ← 21 ways shown in the line above plus 7 new 2-car trains
orange	36 ← 28 ways shown in the line above plus 8 new 2-car trains

Observing how children collect their data, record it, and find patterns can provide you with insights into their problem-solving capacity and learning styles. The ability to make tables and analyze patterns will be highly valued years later when children formally study algebra.

SOLUTION/ NO SOLUTION

Getting Ready

What You'll Need

Cuisenaire Rods, 2 sets per group

1-centimeter grid paper, several sheets per pair, page 110

Crayons

Overhead Cuisenaire Rods and/or 1-centimeter grid paper transparency

Overview

Children decide whether or not puzzles written about Cuisenaire Rods have a solution. If they think there is no solution, children are challenged to explain why no solution is possible. In this activity, children have the opportunity to:

- ◆ use logical reasoning
- ◆ find multiple solutions to a problem

The Activity

Introducing

- ◆ Head two sheets of paper *Puzzles with solutions* and *Puzzles with no solutions*.
- ◆ Give children the following puzzles to solve. Invite volunteers to share the outcome of their work and discuss which puzzles have *just one solution, more than one solution,* or *no solutions.*

  1. Find a rod that is longer than a 2-car train of purple rods and shorter than an orange rod. *(just one solution)*

  2. Find a 2-car train that is as long as a 3-car train made of yellow rods. *(more than one solution)*

  3. Find five rods that cover a 3-by-3-centimeter square. *(more than one solution)*

  4. Find ten rods that cover a 3-by-3-centimeter square. *(no solution)*

- ◆ Have children slide their puzzles onto the appropriate paper.

On Their Own

Which of these Cuisenaire Rod puzzles can be solved? Which cannot?

- Work with a group. Read each puzzle below.

- If a puzzle can be solved, record its solution on grid paper. See if you can find more than one solution for the puzzle.

- If a puzzle cannot be solved, be ready to explain why.

Puzzles

1. Find a rod that is longer than a purple rod but shorter than a brown rod.

2. Find a rod that is shorter than a 2-car train of light green rods and longer than a yellow rod.

3. Find a 3-car train of rods of the same color that is as long as a brown rod.

4. Find a train as long as 3 brown rods using only red and purple rods.

5. Find a square made with 5 rods.

6. Find a square made from 3 rods of each of these colors: white, red, purple, and yellow.

7. Find a 4-car train made from all different-colored rods that is as long as a blue rod.

8. Find a rectangle made from purple rods that covers 20 square centimeters.

9. Find a rectangle made from light green rods that covers 20 square centimeters.

10. Find a train as long as 3 brown rods that is made up of rods of 1 color.

The Bigger Picture

Thinking and Sharing

Write the numbers 1 to 10 across the chalkboard. Have volunteers post their recordings under the corresponding numbers. For each puzzle that they determined to have "no solution," have children discuss why they reached that conclusion.

Use prompts like these to promote class discussion:

- How did you determine if a puzzle had a solution or not?

- How can you use words, instead of rods, to explain why a puzzle has no solution?

- Is it easier to be sure that a puzzle has a solution or does not have a solution? Why?

- For which puzzles was it easy to find solutions? For which was it most difficult?

Writing

Have children choose one of the puzzles with no solution and explain why it did not have a solution.

Teacher Talk

Where's the Mathematics?

A number of the puzzles in this activity have multiple solutions. Children need to find only one solution to classify a puzzle as having a solution. It is a more difficult task to determine that a puzzle has no solution. Encourage children to explain the difference between "impossible to find" and "difficult to find" as they talk about their experiences in trying to solve the puzzles. Children will discover that missing a word, using the wrong color, or substituting "or" for "and" can change the meaning of the puzzle, frustrate them in their search for solutions, and possibly lead them to find incorrect solutions.

The following list indicates sample solutions for some puzzles and explanations of why there are no solutions for others.

1. Find a rod that is longer than a purple rod but shorter than a brown rod.

Three possible solutions: yellow, dark green, or black

2. Find a rod that is shorter than a 2-car train of light green rods and longer than a yellow rod.

There is no solution. The 2-car train is 6 centimeters long and the yellow rod is 5 centimeters long; there is no Cuisenaire Rod with a length between 5 and 6 centimeters.

3. Find a 3-car train of rods of the same color that is as long as a brown rod.

There is no solution. The brown rod is 8 centimeters long, and 8 is not a multiple of 3; or, three red rods would be 1 centimeter short, and three light green rods (the next larger-sized rod) would be 1 centimeter long.

4. Find a train as long as 3 brown rods using only red and purple rods.

There are many solutions. A train of three brown rods is 24 centimeters long. Since red and purple rods have lengths of 2 and 4 centimeters, respectively, there are many ways to combine them to build a train of 24 centimeters. Any train with the following combinations of rods in any order is a solution: two reds and five purples; four reds and four purples; six reds and three purples; eight reds and two purples; ten reds and one purple.

5. Find a square made with 5 rods.

There are solid-square and hollow-square solutions. Some combinations of rods that form solid squares: five yellow rods; one light green, two reds, and two whites. Some examples of hollow squares are shown.

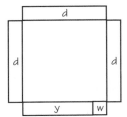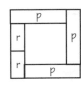

Extending the Activity

1. Ask children to choose one of the "no solution" puzzles and rewrite it so that it will have a solution.

2. Have children work in pairs to create one rod puzzle that has a solution and one puzzle that does not have solution.

---

6. *Find a square made from 3 rods of each of these colors: white, red, purple, and yellow.*

These twelve rods can cover a 36-square-centimeter square, so a solid-square solution would measure 6 centimeters on a side. A variety of solid- and hollow- square solutions can be made, including the following:

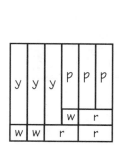 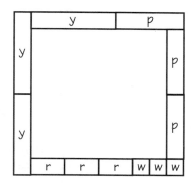

7. *Find a 4-car train made from all different-colored rods that is as long as a blue rod.*

There is no solution because the train formed by each of the four smallest rods has a length equal to that of the orange rod.

8. *Find a rectangle made from purple rods that covers 20 square centimeters.*

There is one solution, the solid rectangle made from five purple rods.

9. *Find a rectangle made from light green rods that covers 20 square centimeters.*

There is no solution because a light green rod covers 3 square centimeters and 20 is not a multiple of 3.

10. *Find a train as long as 3 brown rods that is made up of rods of one color.*

A train of three brown rods is 24 centimeters long. Any rod whose length is a factor of 24 will work, so there are five trains that are solutions: a 24-car train of white rods, a 12-car train of red rods, an 8-car train of light green rods, a 6-car train of purple rods, and a 4-car train of dark green rods.

SQUEEZE PLAY

• Spatial reasoning
• Estimation
• Game strategies

Getting Ready

What You'll Need

Cuisenaire Rods, 1 of each of 10 different colors per child

Squeeze Play game boards, 1 set per pair, pages 99–100

Overhead Cuisenaire Rods and/or *Squeeze Play* game board transparencies (optional)

Overview

In this game for two players, children take turns placing Cuisenaire Rods within a given outline in an attempt to be the last player to place a rod. In this activity, children have the opportunity to:

◆ improve spatial reasoning

◆ develop strategic thinking skills

The Activity

Introducing

◆ Tell children that they will be playing a Cuisenaire Rod game called *Squeeze Play.*

◆ Explain the game rules given in *On Their Own.*

◆ Emphasize that rods may not be moved once they have been placed.

◆ Demonstrate by playing a partial game of *Squeeze Play* either by yourself or with a volunteer.

On Their Own

Play *Squeeze Play!*

Here are the rules.

1. This is a game for 2 players. The object is to be the player who places the last Cuisenaire Rod on the game board.

2. Players choose 1 of the *Squeeze Play* game boards shown below. Each player gets 10 rods, 1 of each color.

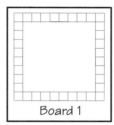
Board 1

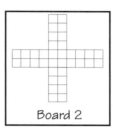
Board 2

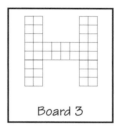
Board 3

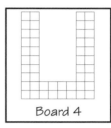
Board 4

3. Players take turns placing the rod of their choice within the grid lines on the game board. Once a rod is placed, it cannot be moved.

4. The player who puts down the last rod is the winner.

- Play several games of *Squeeze Play*. Take turns going first.

- If time permits, choose another game board and play a few more times.

- Be ready to talk about good moves and bad moves.

The Bigger Picture

Thinking and Sharing

Invite children to talk about their games and describe some of the thinking they did.

Use prompts like these to promote class discussion:

- ◆ Did you choose a particular rod to begin play? If so, which one and why?

- ◆ Which rods are the easiest to place? Which are the most difficult? Why?

- ◆ Did you ever place a rod that you wanted to take back? Explain.

- ◆ Is it necessary to think about your partner's remaining rods when you make your choices? Explain.

- ◆ What plan of action did you develop while playing the game?

- ◆ Which game board was the hardest to play on? the easiest? Why?

Writing

Ask children to describe the difference between a game of strategy and a game of chance.

Extending the Activity

1. Challenge the children to design their own *Squeeze Play* game boards. Then have them play the game on their boards.

Where's the Mathematics?

This game can help children develop strategies involving spatial reasoning. Most children will begin playing without a particular strategy in mind. As they continue to play, they will have an opportunity to test different strategies. Children who are familiar with the game of chess may liken *Squeeze Play* to chess by saying, "Just like in chess you have to think ahead so you don't catch yourself in your own trap." As in chess, the offensive player has a better chance of winning than does the defensive player. Generally, the longer that children play, the more time they spend thinking before completing each move in order to survey the pieces their opponent has left and decide how they can use their remaining rods to the best advantage. They learn that as the game progresses, the shorter rods are easier to place than the longer rods, so they learn to save the white, red, and green rods for later in the game.

Some children will report that the placement of a piece is often more important than its length. For example, a player has placed the yellow rod as shown below in order to break up a long column of empty spaces and force the other player to use shorter rods to complete that side of the game board. If the other player had held on to the white, red, and green rods, this placement of the yellow rod would offer places to play these shorter rods. However, if the player had used these shorter rods earlier in the game, the player placing the yellow rod would have won.

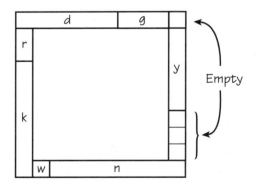

With experience, some children are also able to survey the rods still held by the other player and determine the winner without actually finishing the game. This shows a highly developed level of strategizing since these

2. Have children play again, but this time, the player who puts down the last rod loses.

children are able to play several moves "in their head," anticipating the outcome.

Interestingly enough, there is a winning strategy in this game for each of the first three game boards, but children do not usually discover it because they think it is "copying." The strategy is based on the idea of rotational symmetry. The player who goes second can always win by using the same piece that the first player used in the same position on the board after the board has been rotated 180 degrees around the center.

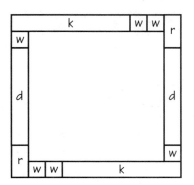 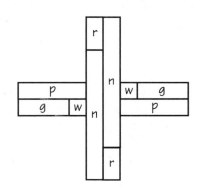 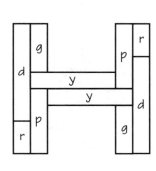

If there is room for the first player's piece, there will always be room for the second player's corresponding piece. When the second player consistently uses the same pieces that the first player did, however, the first player is apt to get testy declaring, that the play is "unfair," and may say, "You can't copy me!" Therefore, this winning strategy is likely to be discovered only if children have discussed their strategies with their partners.

The fourth game board does not have rotational symmetry; it has mirror symmetry. Thus, there is no winning strategy that can be used for this board.

You may find that children are able to play the game thoughtfully but that they cannot articulate their strategies. Do not be discouraged by this. Listening to the children who can explain their strategies may help the more reticent children find the words to express what they have been subconsciously doing.

STAIRCASES

- Patterns
- Estimation
- Addition
- Counting

Getting Ready

What You'll Need

Cuisenaire Rods, 1 set per pair

1-centimeter grid paper, page 110 (optional)

Calculators (optional)

Overhead Cuisenaire Rods and/or 1-centimeter grid paper transparency (optional)

Overview

Children build a staircase with Cuisenaire Rods and extend the patterns they see to find the number of white rods needed to build a staircase of a specified height. In this activity, children have the opportunity to:

- ◆ add and/or multiply numbers through twenty
- ◆ find, describe, and extend patterns

The Activity

Review, or introduce, the numerical value of each rod when the white rod has the value of 1.

Introducing

- ◆ Ask children to use rods to make a staircase. Call on volunteers to share their results.
- ◆ Discuss the pattern used for each staircase and how the staircases are alike and different. If necessary, give examples such as these:

    A goes up by ones, whereas C goes up by twos.
    A and D have the same pattern, but D has an extra step.
    C can be turned to look like B with one less step.

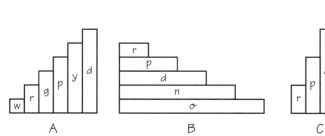

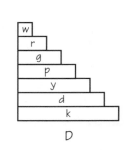

On Their Own

> **How can you find the number of white rods needed for a staircase that would reach up as high as 2 orange rods?**
>
> - Work with a partner. Use Cuisenaire Rods to build a staircase that looks like the one shown here.
>
> - Imagine that the staircase was made of white rods only. Now imagine that it was extended to be as high as 2 orange rods. Estimate how many white rods it would take to build such a staircase. Record your estimate.
>
> - Now find the actual number of white rods it would take to build the extended staircase. Try to find the answer in 2 different ways.
>
> - Record your solutions and be ready to explain them.

w r g p y d k n e o

The Bigger Picture

Thinking and Sharing

Have pairs of children take turns describing how they made their estimate and how they found a solution.

Use prompts such as these to promote class discussion.

- ◆ Was your answer close to your estimate? Explain.

- ◆ What patterns did you find? How were they helpful?

- ◆ If you were to do this problem again with a different staircase, which method of finding the number of white rods would you choose? Why?

Writing

Have children write a set of directions for finding the number of white rods it would take to build a staircase that is two orange rods high.

Extending the Activity

1. Have children find out how many white rods it takes to make a staircase as tall as two orange rods if the staircase begins as shown at right.

2. Display this staircase. Have children find out how many white rods would be needed to extend it so that it is ten layers high.

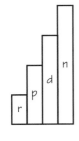

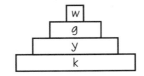

Where's the Mathematics?

Although there is only one numerical answer, 210 white rods, there are many ways to approach this problem. One approach is to look at the staircase as a series of 20 steps, each one unit taller than the previous step. Numerically, this means finding the sum $1 + 2 + 3 + 4 + \ldots + 19 + 20$. If the addends are rearranged like this, $(1 + 20) + (2 + 19) + (3 + 18) + \ldots + (10 + 11)$, ten pairs are formed, each with a sum of 21. Then the result can be found by multiplying 21 by 10.

Another approach is to envision a staircase from 1 to 10, followed by another staircase from 1 to 10 that rests on top of a square that measures 10 x 10 whites, or 100 square centimeters. This would give a total of $55 + 55 + 100$, or 210 white rods.

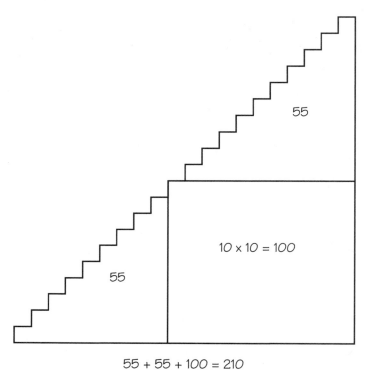

55

$10 \times 10 = 100$

55

$55 + 55 + 100 = 210$

Still another way is to start with the smallest possible staircase and build increasingly larger ones. Recording the total number of steps and the white rods needed for each staircase gives the following results.

Steps	1	2	3	4	5	6	7	8	9	10	11	12	13	14	15	16	17	18	19	20
White rods	1	3	6	10	15	21	28	36	45	55	66	78	91	105	120	136	153	171	190	210

The numbers 1, 3, 6, 10, 15, ... form the sequence of *triangular numbers*. Children may make the observation that this is a growing numerical pattern in which the numbers that are added to get to the next term increase by 1.

It may help some children to understand why the numbers are called triangular by showing them an illustration like this:

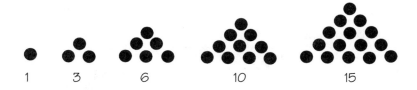

Some children may find that building two staircases and putting them together to form a rectangle is a way to find the total number of white rods needed. These two six-step staircases take the same number of rods. Together, they make a rectangle which takes 6 x 7, or 42, white rods. So each staircase takes 42 ÷ 2, or 21, white rods to build.

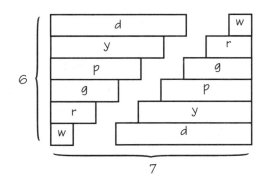

Similarly, placing two seven-step staircases together forms a 7 x 8 rectangle. Therefore, the number of white rods in the seven-step staircase would be (7 x 8) divided by 2, or 28. Continuing this pattern, the number of white rods in the 20-step staircase is (20 x 21) divided by 2, or 210. Children who are ready to think in terms of formulas may understand this generalization: The number of white rods in a staircase of *n* steps (or the *n*th triangular number) is [*n* x (*n* + 1)] ÷ 2.

SYMMETRY SEARCH

• Spatial visualization
• Symmetry

Getting Ready

What You'll Need

Cuisenaire Rods, 1 green and 1 orange per child

Mirrors, 1 per child

Glue stick or clear tape, 1 per child

Symmetry Search worksheet, 1 per child, page 101

Overview

Children figure out where to place a mirror on a given arrangement of Cuisenaire Rods to produce various symmetrical designs. In this activity, children have the opportunity to:

◆ work with reflective and rotational symmetry

◆ determine the effects of moving a line of symmetry

◆ use spatial reasoning

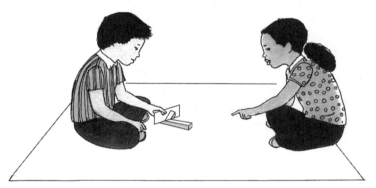

The Activity

Explain that the mirror should be held perpendicular to the light green rod so that it forms a right angle with the rod's top face.

Introducing

◆ Give each child a light green Cuisenaire Rod and a small mirror. Have children rest the mirror on top of the rod so that part of the rod is reflected in the mirror. Allow time for children to explore how changing the placement of the mirror creates different reflections.

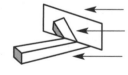

Mirror
Reflected rod
Rod partly hidden beneath mirror

◆ Sketch designs A and B on the chalkboard and challenge children to describe where the mirror could be placed on the light green rod in order to create each one.

A   B

◆ Demonstrate the ways to record how the designs are made and the placement of the mirror for each. Trace around the light green rod, then draw a dashed line to represent the position of the mirror. Add arrows to indicate which side of the mirror has the reflective surface.

◆ Verify that each design can be recorded in a number of ways.

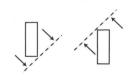

Some solutions for design A

Some solutions for design B

On Their Own

> **Where should you place a mirror on an arrangement of Cuisenaire Rods to create a design?**
>
>
>
> • Work on your own. Glue a light green rod and an orange rod together as shown. Allow a few minutes for the glue to harden.
>
> • Each design on the Symmetry Search worksheet can be made by laying your rod arrangement flat and placing a mirror on it. Find out where the mirror should be placed to make each design.
>
> • Record your solution for each design by tracing around the light green and orange rods and then drawing a dashed line to show where you placed the mirror. Finally, add arrows to show which side of the mirror has the reflective surface. Here is the solution for a U-shaped design.
>
>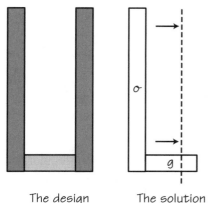
>
> The design   The solution
>
> • With a partner, talk about how you decided where to put the mirror to re-create each design.

The Bigger Picture

Thinking and Sharing

Invite children to share their solutions and talk about what they learned.

Use prompts such as these to promote class discussion:

♦ How did you figure out where to place the mirror to create design number ———?

♦ What clues about mirror placement could you learn from the designs?

♦ Does knowing that a figure has symmetry help you know where to place the mirror? Explain.

♦ Were some designs harder to find solutions for than others? If so, which ones? Why?

♦ Did the solutions to some designs help you find the solutions to others? If so, what was alike about the two designs?

Extending the Activity

Have children find and draw additional designs based on the light-green-and-orange rod arrangement. Then have them exchange their drawings and challenge a partner to find out where the mirror was placed to create their designs.

Where's the Mathematics?

In *Symmetry Search,* children work with congruence, symmetry, rotations, reflections, and visualization of angles and distances. The design that is produced by the mirror has to be exactly the same size and shape as (that is, congruent to) the pictured design. In order to exactly match each design, children may have to rotate the light-green-and-orange rod arrangement before placing the mirror.

The following solutions show the original rod arrangement rotated into position to agree with the orientations of the designs on the *Symmetry Search* worksheet.

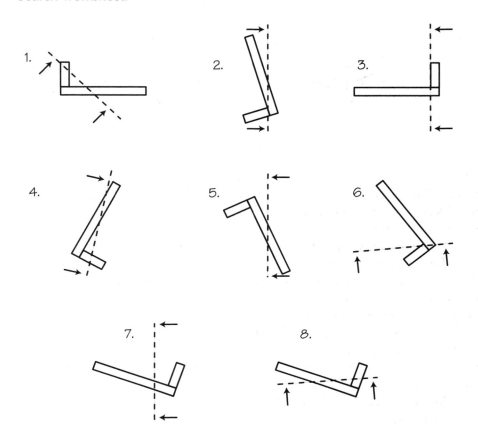

Children intuitively learn that the mirror needs to be placed on the rods at the same angle as the line of symmetry in the design. For example, in Design 6, the line of symmetry makes a 25-degree angle with the side of the design; therefore, the mirror must be placed at a 25-degree angle along the orange rod in the original arrangement.

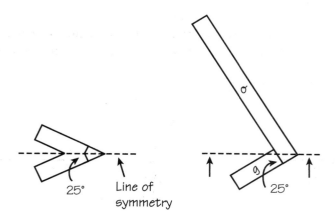

Some children will use a trial-and-error approach all the way through this activity. On the other hand, after drawing the solution for each of the first few designs, some children will begin to see a resemblance between the line of symmetry in the designs and the placement of the mirror on the rods. They may consciously use this idea, rotating the original rod design so that the colors appear to be in the correct locations and then moving the mirror along the design at the same angle as the line of symmetry. In the example involving Design 6, a child might think, "I need to rotate the rod arrangement until the light green is on the left side and the orange is on the right because that is how the light and dark shading appears above and below the line of symmetry in the design. Now I will slide the mirror along so that it's at the same angle as the line of symmetry in the design until the rods and their reflection look just like the design." The child may not use words like "line of symmetry" and "angle," but these are likely to be the ideas he or she is using.

TILING WITH RODS

- Area
- Spatial visualization
- Comparing
- Equivalence

Getting Ready

What You'll Need

Cuisenaire Rods, 2 sets per pair

Floor Plan Cards 1–4, 1 set per pair, pages 102–105

Overhead Cuisenaire Rods and/or Floor Plan cards transparencies (optional)

Overview

Children estimate, compare, and measure area by filling outlines of polygons with Cuisenaire Rods. In this activity, children have the opportunity to:

- build an understanding of area
- learn that different shapes can have the same area
- find area in terms of different units of measure

The Activity

Introducing

- Show children the outlines of two rectangles but do not tell them the dimensions. Rectangle A should measure 4-by-5 centimeters and Rectangle B should measure 3-by-6 centimeters.

- Ask children to imagine that these rectangles are the floors of two classrooms that you want to cover with tiles. Ask which room they think will need more tiles and why.

- Invite volunteers to cover each rectangle with red rods. Ask the class to tell which shape is bigger and why.

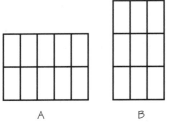

A
Area = 10 red rods

B
Area = 9 red rods

On Their Own

Which room has the larger floor?

- Work with a partner. Choose a Floor Plan card. On each card, 2 of the floors have the same area and 1 of the floors is larger.

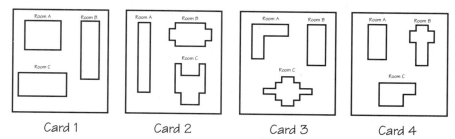

Card 1 Card 2 Card 3 Card 4

- Use Cuisenaire Rods to find the area of each floor. Keep track of the rods you use and the number of each.

- Figure out which floor is larger. Think of ways to describe how much larger it is than the other floors.

- Repeat the activity with the other Floor Plan cards.

The Bigger Picture

Thinking and Sharing

Take one card at a time and invite children to discuss how they found the sizes of the floors on that card. As children discuss results, record on the board the number and color of the rods that children used.

Use prompts like these to promote class discussion.

- ◆ What method did you use for comparing the floors of the rooms?

- ◆ Which floor is bigger? How do you know? How much bigger is it? Did anyone have a different answer? What is it?

- ◆ Here is one set of rods that covers Floor (name a letter) and here is a different set of rods that also covers it. Does this mean the same floor has two different sizes? Explain.

- ◆ Would one rod be better than any other rod for comparing the sizes of different floors? Is so, which rod and why?

Extending the Activity

1. Explain that the word *area* is used to describe how much surface a figure covers. Introduce the term *square centimeter* (the area of one face of the white Cuisenaire Rod) as one of the units that is used to measure area. Have children find the area of each room in square centimeters.

2. Have children make up more examples of "Floor Plan" cards and use them to challenge other children to find the areas of the floors.

Where's the Mathematics?

Through their investigations in *Tiling with Rods,* children build an intuitive understanding of area and how to measure it. This understanding can make their subsequent studies of area formulas more meaningful.

Although each "Floor Plan" card has only one correct answer, this activity is open-ended in the sense that children use a variety of methods for measuring area, comparing the areas, and arriving at a final answer. Repeating the activity with several different Floor Plan cards allows children to apply what they have just learned to a slightly different situation and further refine their problem-solving approach.

Children see that a variety of rods can be used to cover the outlines on each Floor Plan card. They come to see that a meaningful comparison of areas can be made if one unit is consistently used to measure each of the outlines on the card. For example, on card 1, children might begin by covering Room A with 5 dark green rods, Room B with 10 green rods, and Room C with 4 brown rods. Since the rods are of different lengths, comparing the numbers 5, 10, and 4 does not give a meaningful answer. Some children may then decide to start all over again and try to cover all three rectangles with the same-colored rod. Others, however, may decide to start "trading in" rods. For example, these children may physically or mentally remove one dark green rod from Room A and trade it in for two light green rods continuing in this way until they have replaced the 5 dark greens with 10 light green rods. At this point, some children will use the logic that if Rooms A and B both require 10 light green rods, then Room C must the one with the different (larger) area. Other children will need to replace all the rods on Room C with light green ones to discover that it has room for 10 light green rods and two more empty spaces. These children may reason that Room C must have the larger area. Other children may still be unconvinced and will continue to work until they have completely covered all three rooms on the card with the same colored rods.

As they move from card to card, some children use the experience they gained from previous cards and may decide that using the same-colored rod on all of the rooms makes the most sense. They may also see that choosing a shorter rod, such as red or white, is more likely to guarantee that the room can be completely covered.

Some children will use the strategy of covering each room completely with a collection of different-colored rods and then placing the rods for each room end-to-end, comparing the length of the trains to determine which is longer. Children who are proficient with computation may use this idea symbolically and translate all the rods in the trains into their numerical values. They then find the area of each by finding the sum of the numerical values of the rods in each train.

Asking children to decide whether two seemingly different measurements are really the same is apt to lead to a discussion of expressing all areas on a card in terms of one type of Cuisenaire rod so that comparisons may be more easily made. This may lead them to discover and use the relationships among the rods. For example, children who began by using many different-colored rods and then decided to express their answers using only red rods may realize that they could convert their original answers to red rods without beginning all over and re-covering the room with red rods. For example, if they used 3 browns and recognize that 4 reds equal a brown, they can use addition or multiplication to find that the area covered by 3 browns is equivalent to the area covered by 12 red rods.

The idea that 3 browns covers the same area as 12 reds is an example of equivalence, a key idea in mathematics. You can help children make the connection between equivalence in this activity and in their other math studies by pointing out, for example, that two feet is the same as 24 inches because each foot is equivalent to 12 inches.

When asked if one rod would be better than any other rod for comparing the sizes of different floors, children are likely to conclude that the smallest rod, the white one, would be the best. This is because every floor can be covered with white rods with no leftover, uncovered spaces. Listening to one another explain their strategies in approaching this problem, children can gain an appreciation of the fact that there can be many different ways to arrive at a correct answer.

TOUR OF THE ISLANDS

Getting Ready

What You'll Need

Cuisenaire Rods, 1 set per group

Island Map to be taped together, 1 per group, pages 106-109

Crayons

Centimeter ruler, 1 for *Introducing*

Overview

In this game for two to four players, children estimate distances on a map in terms of centimeters or as a combination of various Cuisenaire Rods. They then check their estimates by making trains of rods on the map. In this activity, children have the opportunity to:

◆ estimate and measure with centimeters

◆ do mental computation

◆ strengthen their number sense

The Activity

You may wish to have children play the game without referring to centimeters.

Introducing

◆ Explain to children that Cuisenaire Rods can be used to measure distances in terms of centimeters. Hold a white rod against a centimeter ruler to show that the white rod is one centimeter long. Ask children to determine the lengths of the other rods in centimeters.

◆ Once the lengths of the rods have been established, challenge pairs of children to each place their two index fingers nine centimeters apart on the desktop. Then have them check their estimates with a blue rod.

◆ Ask children to tell which rods could be used to check longer distances, such as 20 centimeters. Accept any reasonable answers, such as using a two-car orange train or two blue rods plus a red rod.

◆ Have children continue to work in pairs, using their index fingers on the desktop to estimate distances between 1 and 30 centimeters and checking their estimates with rods.

◆ Explain the rules for the *Tour of the Islands* game as described in *On Their Own*. Show how to attach the four parts of the map to make up the game board. Then play part of a game with a volunteer.

On Their Own

Play *Tour of the Islands!*

Here are the rules.

1. This is a game for 2 to 4 players. The object is to be the first to land on each of the islands on the game board and then return to the Mainland.

2. Players work on a game board map that shows the Mainland and 6 islands. They decide who goes first. Each player chooses a different-color crayon to record his or her plays.

3. The first player puts an X anywhere on the Mainland to mark a starting point and decides which island to visit first.

4. The player announces an estimate of the distance on the map from the starting point to the island. Then, starting at the X, the player lays down a train of Cuisenaire Rods equal to the estimate so that the train extends in the direction of the first island. The player then marks where the train ends.

   - If the train reaches the island, on the next turn the player can proceed in the same way to any other island.
   - If the train does not reach the island, the player must "tread water" and try to reach the island from this location on the next turn.

5. Players take turns. Each player chooses a different starting point on the Mainland, marks it with an X, and follows the same procedure to go from island to island in any order.

6. When players have visited all the islands, they use the same procedure to return to their starting point on the Mainland.

7. The player who returns to the starting point first is the winner.

- Play the game several times. Visit the islands in a different order each time.

The Bigger Picture

Thinking and Sharing

Invite children to talk about their games and describe some of the thinking they did.

Use prompts like these to promote class discussion:

- Did your estimates get better as you played? Explain.
- Was it easier to accurately estimate short distances or long distances? Why?
- What tips could you give classmates who want to improve their estimates?

Writing

Ask children to choose two islands on the map and write a set of directions for how to estimate and find the distance between them.

Teacher Talk

Where's the Mathematics?

Most children find the game of *Tour of the Islands* an engaging way to practice estimation skills and develop better number sense. Children whose estimation skills improve dramatically while playing this game frequently report that they form a mental image of one of the Cuisenaire Rods, such as the orange, and then use this as a benchmark for making their estimates. They visualize placing these rods end-to-end and make adjustments when the rod trains fall short of or overshoot the desired goal.

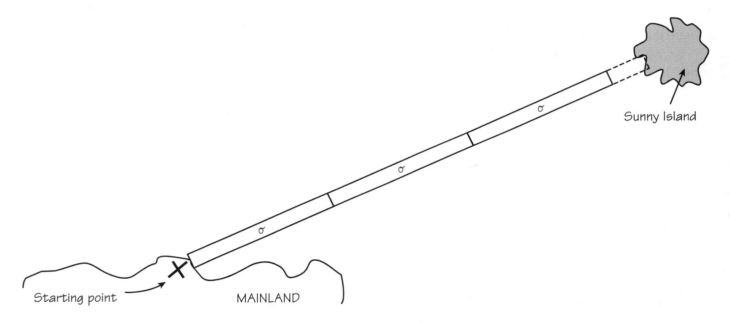

Some children report that they improved their estimating by using measurements they made earlier in the game to help them estimate new distances. For example, if they found that the distance from the mainland to the first island is 28 centimeters and the distance to the second island looks about one and one-half times as far, they estimated that the second distance will measure 28 + 14, or 42, centimeters.

Most children report that the shorter distances are easier to estimate than the longer distances. When they try to estimate a longer distance by mentally

Extending the Activity

1. Have children design their own *Tour of the Islands* game-board maps and play the game again on their maps.

2. Have children keep a running total of the number of centimeters they "travel" in their tour. The winner might then be the player who takes either the longest or shortest tour.

---

making a train of orange rods and then make a mistake in imagining the length of the orange rod, the mistake becomes compounded. Shorter distances, however, require that children visualize the lengths of only one or two rods, so the effects of potential mistakes tend to be minimized.

Once children make their estimate, they need to figure out a train of rods whose lengths will equal that estimate. Many children will accomplish this through multiplication, thinking, "I have estimated 20 centimeters, which could be 4 times 5, or 4 yellow rods." Others think in terms of place value, "I have estimated 23 centimeters, which would be 2 orange (10-centimeter) rods and 3 white (1-centimeter) rods." Still other children just pick up a combination of rods that will add up to the given number, "I have estimated 17 centimeters, which could be a blue (9) plus a brown (8)." Sometimes, you will see children use subtraction as well, reasoning, "I have estimated 39 centimeters, which is almost 40, so if I put down 4 orange rods and then count back one white rod, it will be the same as 39." Observing how their teammates use the rods to check their estimates will give children different strategies for thinking about numbers.

After they have played the game and understand the rules, children enjoy devising ways to make the game more challenging. Some suggest making the islands even smaller and farther apart. The smaller island makes a smaller target to hit, and longer distances are harder to estimate. Some combine the idea of smaller islands with the idea of more islands so that more stops must be made. Some children suggest hiding the rods while the estimate is being made so that players do not have a visual way of checking their measurements. A few children may suggest keeping track of their estimates on a separate piece of paper and adding them to find the total distance of the trip. Then the one with the longest (or shortest, depending on their pre-agreement) trip wins. Some add details, such as sharks and enemy submarines, that must be avoided, challenging players to route their travels around them. Still others add rewards, such as a pirate's chest, and if a player lands exactly on one of these rewards, he or she gets an extra turn or gets to skip to the next island without estimating. The number of variations is limited only by the creativity of the children.

WRITING EQUATIONS

- Addition
- Equations

Getting Ready

What You'll Need

Cuisenaire Rods, 2 reds, 2 light green, 1 purple, and 1 yellow per pair

Strips of paper, 10 cm by 4 cm, at least 10 strips per pair, cut from 1-centimeter grid paper, page 110

Overhead Cuisenaire Rods and/or 1-centimeter grid paper transparency (optional)

Overview

Children work with a specified group of Cuisenaire Rods and explore the many different equations they can represent with them. In this activity, children have an opportunity to:

- write addition sentences
- use the properties of addition and equality

The Activity

Introducing

- Invite a volunteer to build and display a train using two or three rods.

- Invite another volunteer to build another train that is equal in length to the first one. At this point, the trains might look like these:

w	g	p
y	g	

- Ask children to describe how the two trains are related. Have them use letter names for the rods, addition signs, and an equal sign. Children may suggest an equation like this:

$$w + g + p = y + g$$

- Then rearrange the rods in each train and ask children to write equations that reflect the new arrangements.

y	g
w	g	p

(top and bottom trains interchanged)
$$y + g = w + g + p$$

p	g	w
g	y	

(order of rods within each train reversed)
$$p + g + w = g + y$$

On Their Own

How many different equations can you find using a certain group of Cuisenaire Rods?

- Work with a partner. Use these Cuisenaire Rods: 2 reds, 2 light greens, 1 purple, and 1 yellow.

- Choose any of the rods to form 2 trains that are equal in length. Here is an example of a 1-car train equal in length to a 2-car train.

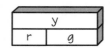

$$y = r + g \qquad r + g = y$$
$$y = g + r \qquad g + r = y$$

- Write as many equations as you can that describe how the two trains are related. Write each equation on its own strip of paper.

- Continue forming trains of equal length and writing equations.

- Find as many different pairs of equal-length trains as you can and record the matching equations.

The Bigger Picture

Thinking and Sharing

Make and post the following four labels: *3 rods, 4 rods, 5 rods, 6 rods.* Ask volunteers, one pair at a time, to post an equation that uses only three rods. Once children agree that there are no duplicates, ask for four-rod equations. Continue in this manner until all the different equations that the class has found are posted.

Use prompts like these to promote class discussion:

- What did you notice about the posted equations?
- How did you use the rods to help you find equations?
- Once you found an equation, could you change it to come up with another one? How?
- Do you think you have found all of the possible equations? Why?
- Did you organize your search in any special way? Explain.
- Which equations represent the same set of rods?

Extending the Activity

1. Have children repeat the activity with fewer than six rods.
2. Have children repeat the activity with different collections of six rods. Have them compare their results with the results of the original activity.

Where's the Mathematics?

As children complete this activity they can deepen their understanding of properties of addition by applying them to the search for new sentences. Some children may use the rods to build every sentence; others may not actually use the rods at all but may manipulate symbols to make new sentences. For example, having found one equation, $r + g = y$, they can use their understanding of the commutative property of addition to find the sentence $g + r = y$. If children think of the equal sign (=) as meaning "the same as," they can justify rewriting $r + g = y$ as $y = r + g$—an illustration of the symmetric property of equality. Again applying the symmetric property, a fourth equation can be written; that is, if $g + r = y$, then $y = g + r$.

There are 46 possible equations. It is unlikely that an individual pair of children—or even the whole class—will find all the sentences. Sorting the equations according to the number of rods used can help children to see what is missing.

There are 6 equations using three rods. These fall into two "families of equations," one family involving r, g, y and the other involving r, r, p:

$r + g = y$	$r + r = p$
$g + r = y$	$p = r + r$
$y = r + g$	
$y = g + r$	

There are 16 equations using four rods: eight involving r, g, p, y; four involving r, r, g, g; and four involving r, g, g, p:

$r + y = g + p$	$r + g = g + r$	$r + p = g + g$
$r + y = p + g$	$r + g = r + g$	$p + r = g + g$
$y + r = g + p$	$g + r = r + g$	$g + g = r + p$
$y + r = p + g$	$g + r = g + r$	$g + g = p + r$
$g + p = r + y$		
$g + p = y + r$		
$p + g = r + y$		
$p + g = y + r$		

There are 24 equations using five rods: twelve involving r, r, g, g, p; and twelve involving r, r, g, p, y.

$p + g = g + r + r$	$y + g = r + r + p$
$p + g = r + g + r$	$y + g = r + p + r$
$p + g = r + r + g$	$y + g = p + r + r$
$g + p = g + r + r$	$g + y = r + r + p$
$g + p = r + g + r$	$g + y = r + p + r$
$g + p = r + r + g$	$g + y = p + r + r$
$g + r + r = p + g$	$r + r + p = y + g$
$g + r + r = g + p$	$r + r + p = g + y$
$r + g + r = p + g$	$r + p + r = y + g$
$r + g + r = g + p$	$r + p + r = g + y$
$r + r + g = p + g$	$p + r + r = y + g$
$r + r + g = g + p$	$p + r + r = g + y$

In the 46 equations above, the sum of the rods from both sides of the equal sign is equivalent to an even number of white rods; this allows half to be on one side of the equal sign and half on the other side. There are no sentences that involve all six rods because the sum of these rods is equivalent to 19 white rods, and it is impossible to form two trains of the same length from 19 white rods.

The process of searching for all the equations involves making a systematic listing; this is the kind of thinking used to solve permutation problems such as, "How many different ways can three textbooks—a math book, a science book, and a history book—be arranged on a bookshelf?" A systematic approach can enhance children's ability to reason mathematically. Using letters to represent the rods provides an exposure to the kind of symbolic thinking children will use in algebra.

CLUE SETS 1 AND 2

Make a rectangle. Set 1	Use 5 rods in all. Set 1
1 rod is purple. Set 1	4 rods have the same color. Set 1

Don't use yellow. Set 2	Use 2 of each color. Set 2
Use 4 rods. Set 2	Make a train that is as long as an orange rod. Set 2

CLUE SETS 3 AND 4

The shape has line symmetry. Set 3	Each rod touches only 2 others. Set 3
Use 3 colors and 6 rods. Set 3	No 2 rods of the same color touch. Set 3

Use 5 rods. Set 4	All the rods are different. Set 4
1 rod is yellow. Set 4	Make a solid rectangle. Set 4

Make a triangle.

Set 5

All sides have
the same length.

Set 5

Use 4 rods.

Set 5

1 rod is purple.

Set 5

Make a square.

Set 6

Use 6 rods.

Set 6

At least 2 of the rods
are the same color.

Set 6

The sides are as
long as a black rod.

Set 6

Draw a banana peel (🍌) in one of the squares.

Draw a banana peel (🍌) in one of the squares.

Draw a banana peel (🍌) in one of the squares.

Draw a banana peel (🍌) in one of the squares.

RODTANGLES GRIDS

Name _____

Name _____

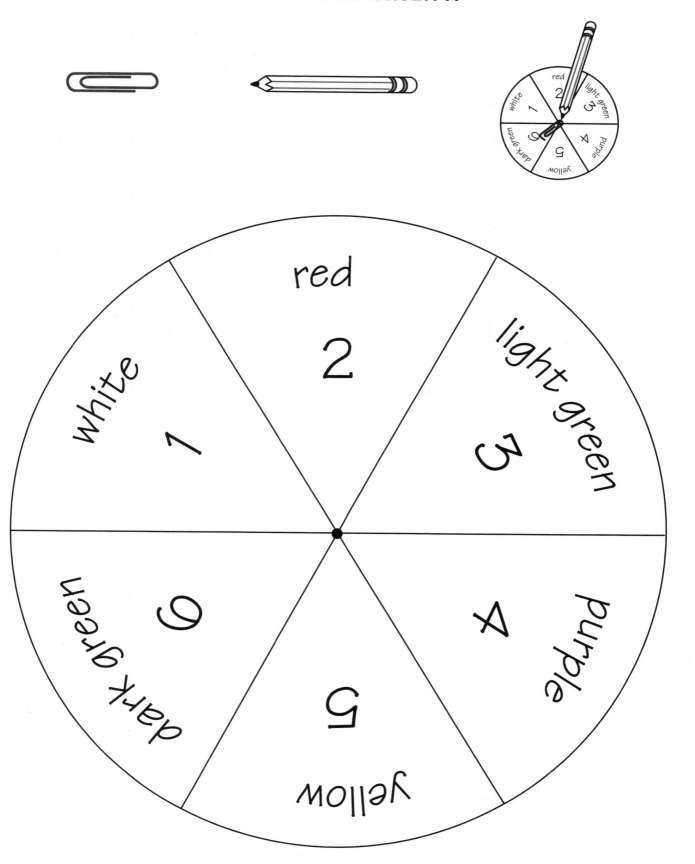

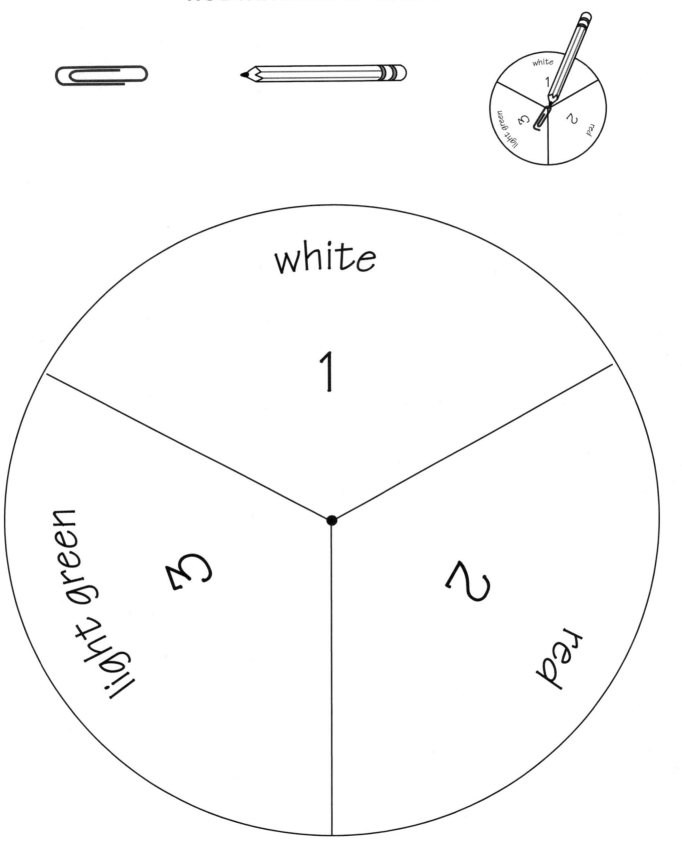

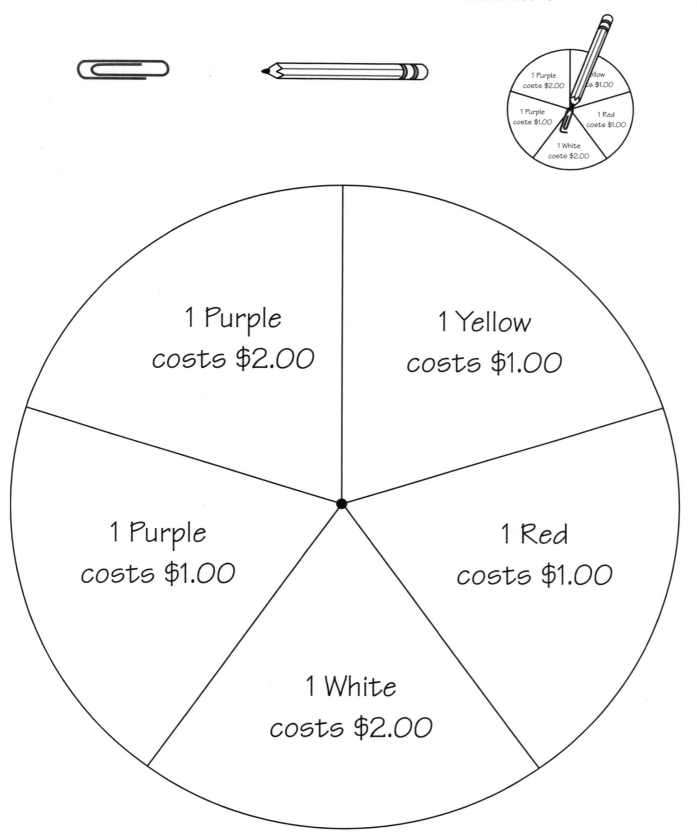

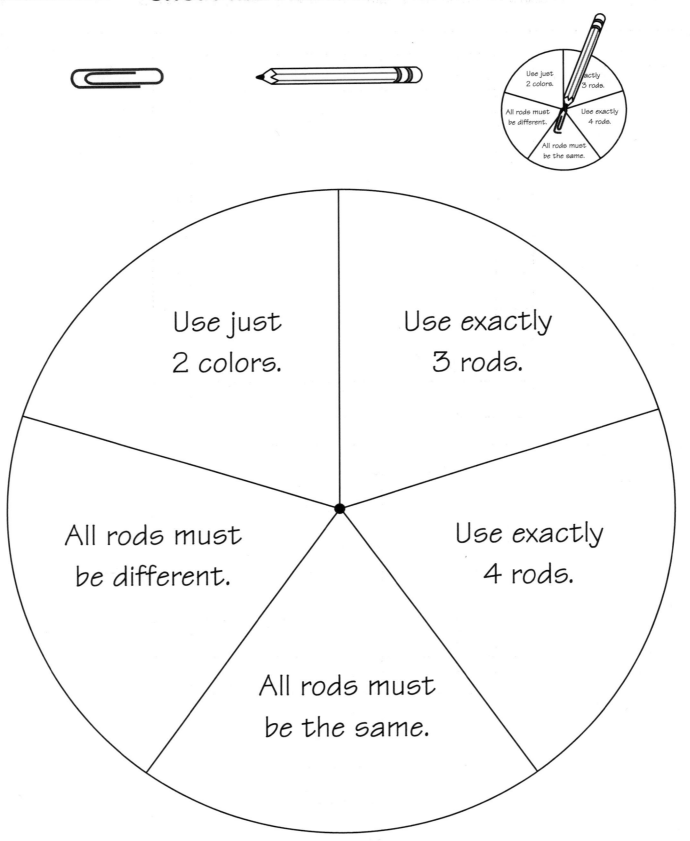

Use just
2 colors.

Use exactly
3 rods.

All rods must
be different.

Use exactly
4 rods.

All rods must
be the same.

Board 1

Board 2

Board 3

Board 4

Each of these designs can be made by placing a mirror on your original green-and-orange rod arrangement.

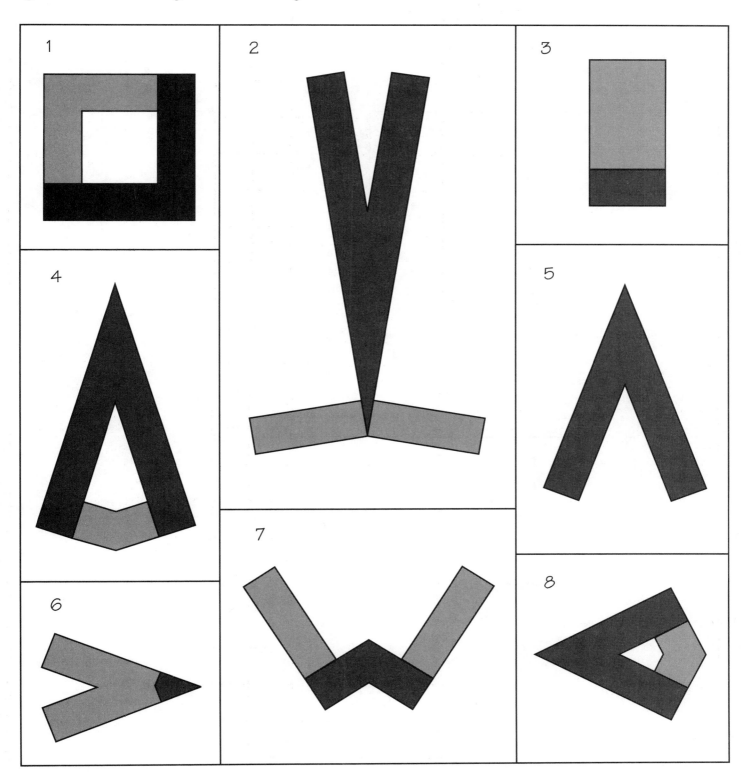

Room A

Room B

Room C

CARD 1

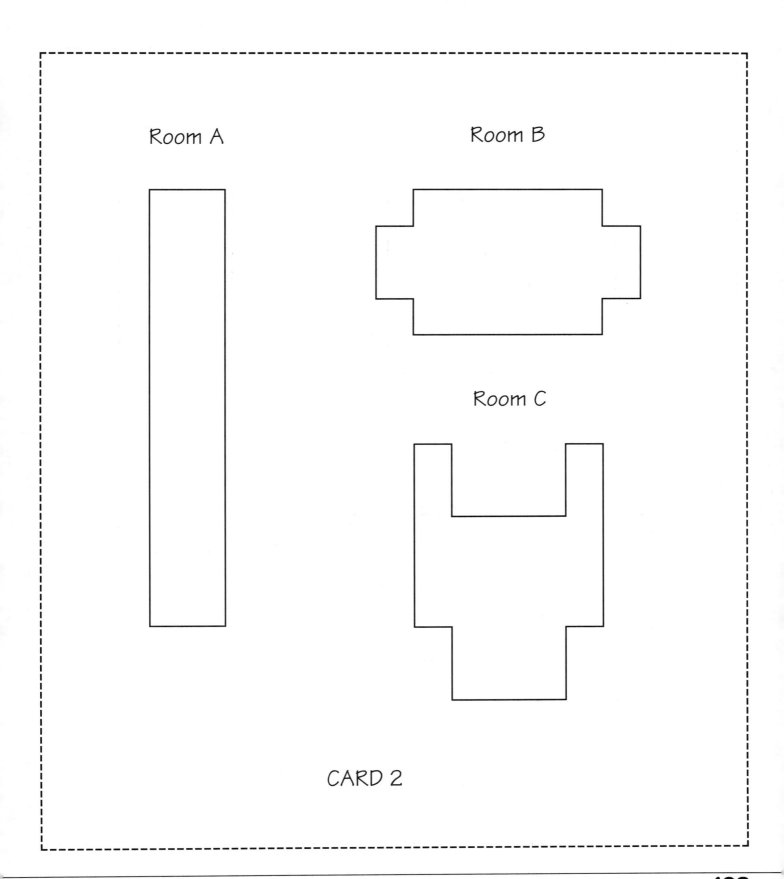

Room A

Room B

Room C

CARD 2

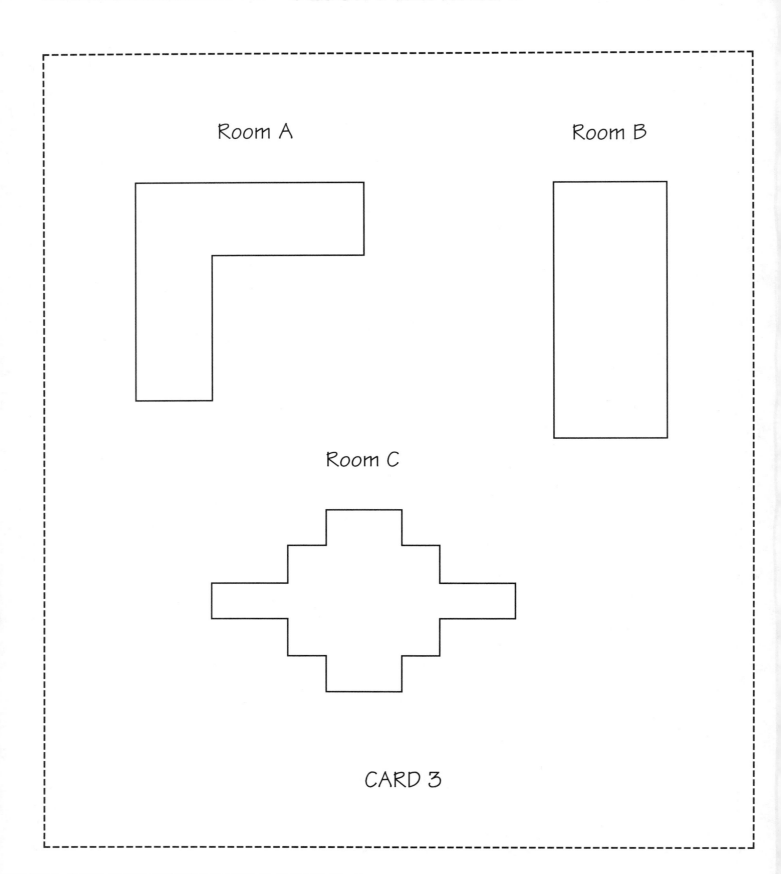

Room A

Room B

Room C

CARD 3

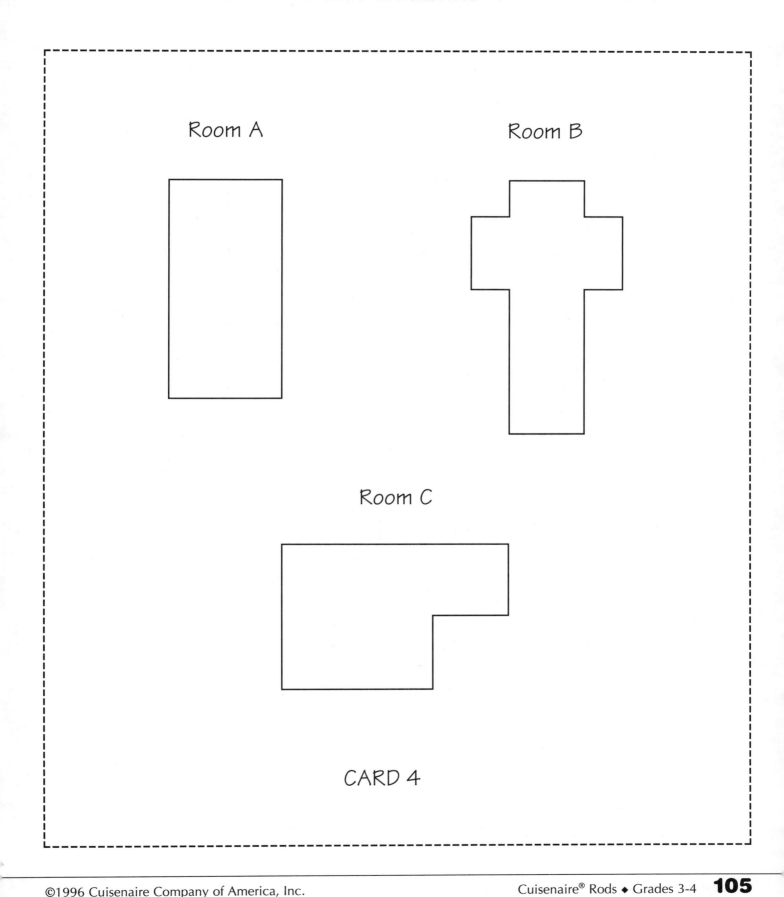

Room A

Room B

Room C

CARD 4

ISLAND MAP
(NORTHWEST SECTION)

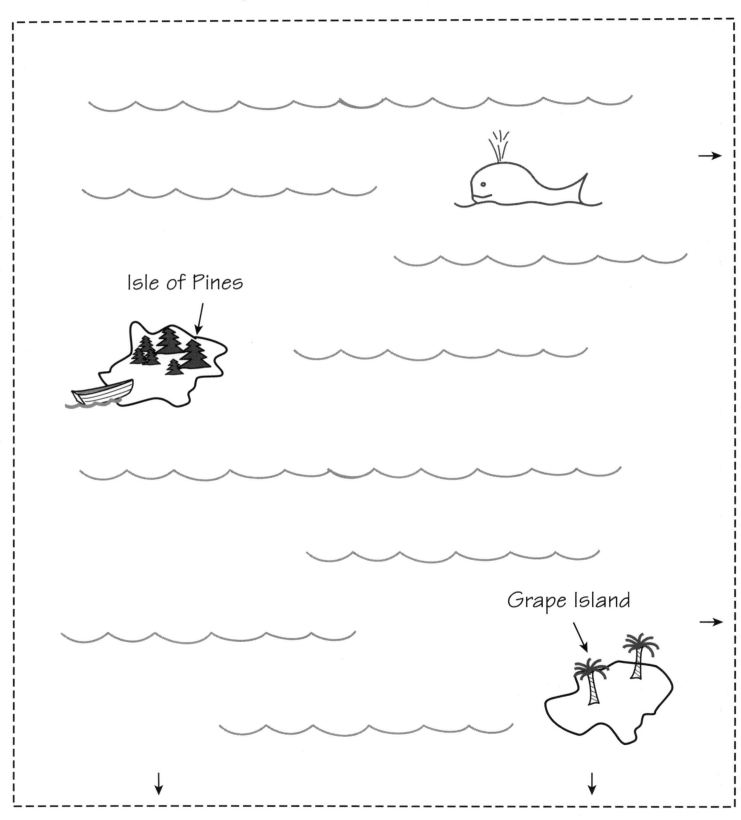

Isle of Pines

Grape Island

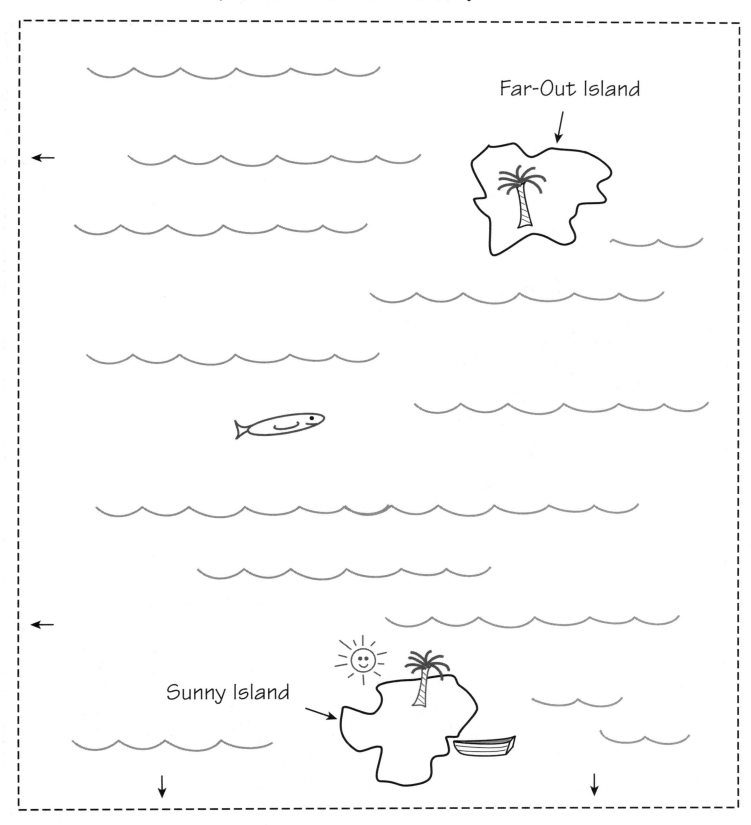

Far-Out Island

Sunny Island

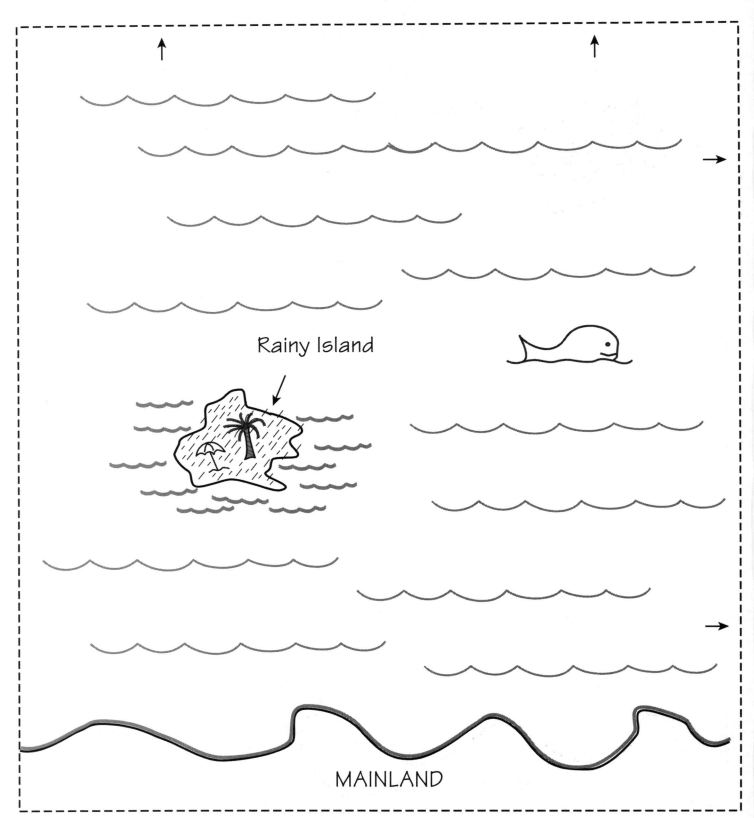

Rainy Island

MAINLAND

ISLAND MAP
(SOUTHEAST SECTION)

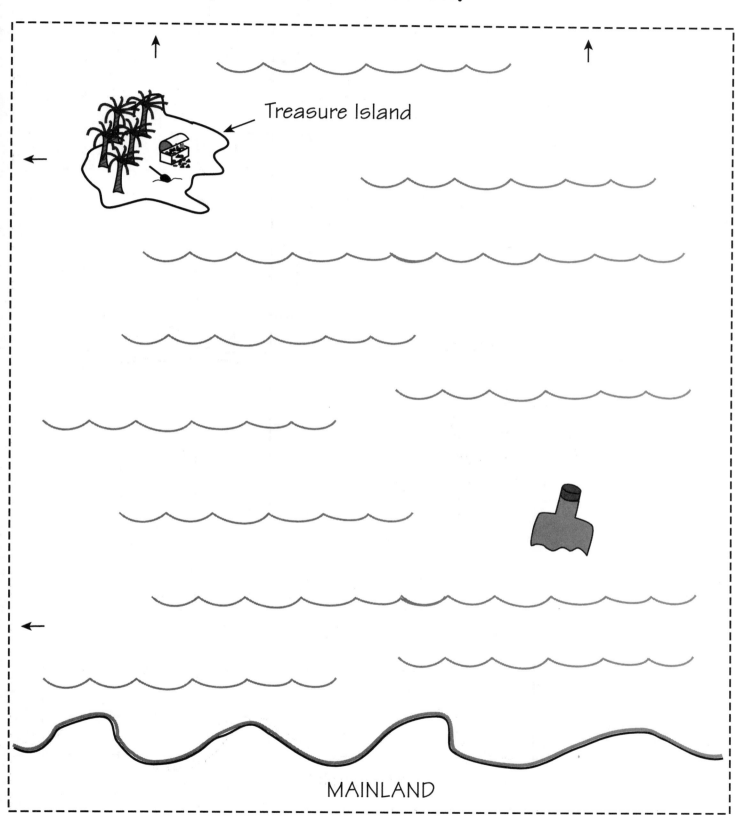

Treasure Island

MAINLAND

CUISENAIRE ROD WRITING PAPER

the Super Source ◆ Cuisenaire® Rods ◆ Grades 3-4